I AM REVIVAL

Preparation Guide for Revival Ready People

Dana M. Blue

BluePrint, A Division of BlueMuse Inspired LLC & Dana Blue Ministries

Copyright © 2023 Dana Blue

All rights reserved. No part of this publication may be reproduced or transmitted in any form or by any means without prior written permission.

This book or parts thereof may not be reproduced in any form, stored in a retrieval system, or transmitted in any form by any means-electronic, mechanical, photocopy, recording or otherwise-without prior written permission of the publisher except as provided by the United States of America copyright law.

Scripture quotations marked (KJV) are taken from the King James Version Bible. Accessed on Bible Gateway. www.biblegateway.com

Scripture quotations marked (NKJV) are taken from the New King James Version Bible. Accessed on Bible Gateway. www.biblegateway.com

Scripture quotations marked (NIV) are taken from the New International Version Bible. Accessed on Bible Gateway. www.biblegateway.com

Scripture quotations marked (AMP) are taken from the Amplified Bible. Accessed on Bible Gateway. www.biblegateway.com

Scripture quotations marked (MSG) are taken from the The Message Bible. Accessed on Bible Gateway. www.biblegateway.com

Scripture quotations marked (CEB) are taken from the The Common English Bible. Accessed on Bible Gateway. www.biblegateway.com

While the author has made every effort to provide accurate internet addresses at the time of publication, neither the publisher nor the author assumes any responsibility for errors or for changes that occur after publication. Further, the publisher does not have any control over and does not assume any responsibility for author or third-party websites or their content.

This book is dedicated to the memory of my mother, Bonzie Morris. Her character, nature, and love prepared me to be the woman I have become. Her legacy lives strong in me.

This book is written to stir the heart of every believer who senses the fire burning deep within to be a GLORY CARRIER, CHANGE AGENT, TRAILBLAZER, and REVIVALIST in the earth.

May you find the divine impetus from within these pages to acknowledge that inner calling and respond with purpose, action, and dedication to doing all that the Father has given you to do!

The time is here! The time is now to boldly proclaim, "I Am Revival"!

ACKNOWLEDGEMENTS

I honor and dedicate this book to my husband, Bishop Mitchel Blue, and my daughters. Their continual support, love, and flexibility have been the impetus I needed to do the things God has called me to do.

I am forever grateful. Mitchel, thanks for the sacrifices you make daily, and for being the one that pushes, affirms, challenges and takes care of me wholeheartedly...you are my forever love. To my daughters, thanks for being so amazing...I love you dearly and I am so excited about your future! You are brilliant, anointed and amazing! I thank God for each of you and the blessing you are to me!

I honor and appreciate my parents; I'm thankful for the life lessons, love, and example of serving you set before me. Thanks for the deposits that continue to shape and inform who I am.

To my brothers, William and Greg...I love you dearly. To my sister, Sharon, thanks for being the best "bossy" sister! I love and appreciate you, and I am thankful for who you are, and all God will do through you.

To Uncommon Church...thank you for the continual support and freedom you provide. It allows me to be who God has uniquely called me to be. You have remained faithful as we all endure the growth and transformation process that will allow us to rise up and boldly and declare, "I AM REVIVAL"!

CONTENTS

Title Page
Copyright
Dedication
Acknowledgements
Foreward
Foreward
Chapter One … 1
Chapter Two … 7
Chapter Three … 23
Chapter Four … 44
Chapter Five … 53
Chapter Six … 65
Chapter Seven … 74
Chapter Eight … 88
Chapter Nine … 101
Chapter Ten … 110
Chapter Eleven … 120
Fourteen Days of Revival Prayer … 130
References … 145
About The Author … 149

Books By This Author   151
Praise For Author   157

FOREWARD

This isn't just another book about Revival, nor is it just another book about healing and change. It's a book for those who are willing to endure the process of heart transformation for this last move of God. I'm excited about writing this foreword for Pastor Dana Blue, a young woman of God that I have had the privilege of mentoring over twenty years and have truly seen the anointing and power of God upon her life.

Dana Blue has captured the heart of God to articulate this last day move before He returns. God is doing mighty works in believers everywhere. As we give the Lord entrance into our lives, He is changing us. In this very timely book you will learn, understand why, and how to have the heart cry of the revivalist. Pastor Dana has set the stage for the ordinary believer to move with the heart of God concerning revival within and not just within our church services but with outward revival.

Every believer should prepare to do the work for the kingdom of God. Pastor Dana said "we carry the breath of revival the winds of change in our being." That is awesome! In our being, inside you, you have the equipping ability to shift atmospheres, change lives and much more.

As I read her book she navigated as pastor, teacher, prophet, counselor and mentor in the process assigned throughout the pages. Yes, it is a process, but one that will produce the outcome of a proven vessel. This process will also qualify you for the mighty signs and wonders that will come forth through you as an agent of change, a revivalist.

This book will engage every reader, but more important, allow you to see and experience change inwardly and right before your eyes! Pastor Dana writing from her experience as a pastor and kingdom leader exercising oversight over the souls of believers systematically, allows her to take the reader on a glorious adventure in the Spirit.

You will enjoy this book as you glean from its different dynamics of spiritual equipping that will propel you into a greater devotion and commitment to the Lord. I recommend it to all believers, especially to Leaders in the Body of Christ to help the people under your leadership excel as a Revivalist' Change Agents. I also recommend it to Christian Bible Colleges and Universities. I'm grateful to God and Pastor Dana about what's about to happen to all believers that read and apply the message that is in this book.

Dr. Apostle Beverly Smith, Founder and President of
Beverly Smith Ministries; Throne of His Glory Summits

FOREWARD

There are questions that have beleaguered the church for years surrounding the subject of revival. What is a "fire starter"? What exactly causes the flames of revival to hit a church, city, or region? What are the hindrances to revival? How does the revivalist survive the hits from the enemy simply because they are chosen? How can you have a sustainable revival and grow healthy emerging people?

This book, I AM REVIVAL, is indeed A MODEL OF TRANSFORMATION FOR TODAYS REVIVALIST, is a total game changer. Having read many works on revival throughout my career, this book joins the ranks of significant revivalists of years gone by, like Leonard Ravenhill and Charles Spurgeon. There is a longing deep in man's heart to have uninterrupted communion with the Father and to be used by God to impact lives with holiness and wholeness. This book stirs up the passion for that higher-level pursuit of God.

Dana Blue looks at key elements of past revivals and what it will take for us to revisit those refreshing times and re-dig the wells of our fathers. God created Israel as a paradigmatic people. He established a worship calendar with sacred feasts and holy days to remind Israel that their lives were to be built around Him. There was a constant pulling us back to the presence of the Father because man is prone to wander. The underlying theme of the book is the roadmap to our return to the presence of God. Revival carves out a unique place for God to settle. It not only brings visitation, but it also brings habitation.

In this book, we discover the spotlight that revival puts on our souls. Revival exposes us to ourselves and makes us deal with the ugly parts of our hearts. It also gently nudges us to the possibilities of the future as God speaks and makes known His plan. The words on every page will fully engage you until you ask God to heal your soul, heal your heart, and make you His instrument. This book seems to be our 911 call for Heaven's immediate response. We know that if God is the same today as He was yesterday, He's ready to heal and deliver.

I salute Prophet Dana Blue for penning the thoughts of God as the Spirit breathed them on her. I encourage you to keep pressing in. This book will have your heart leaping from beginning to end, asking God to give you revival. As you go through these pages, do so with Bible, pen, and Kleenex. The Bible will confirm what God is saying; the pen is for the myriad of thoughts that will flood your mind, and Kleenex is to help you wipe the tears as they are bound to fall. Let the journey begin.

Bishop Randy Borders, Harvest Church Ministries Intl.

Revival is a renewed conviction of sin and repentance, followed by an intense desire to live in obedience to God. It is giving up one's will to God in deep humility.

CHARLES G. FINNEY

CHAPTER ONE

#Marked

The instructions of the Lord are perfect, reviving the soul. The decrees of the Lord are trustworthy, making wise the simple. Psalms 19:7

Jesus and Church have always been a part of my life. I was born in a Christian home and hailed from three generations of Pastors. The year that I was born was the same year that my father accepted his calling and then went into ministry as a bi-vocational pastor.

Growing up, I always felt a deep understanding of spiritual things. There was a season in my youth when I became very acquainted with the dark side of the spiritual realm as the enemy attempted to introduce different doors to the Kingdom of darkness. I was tormented through dreams (night terrors) while, at the same time, I was fascinated with spirituality overall. I embodied an innate ability to see and understand things (discernment) and know things others did not. Sometimes, I walk to the beat of not necessarily my own drum but definitely a different drum. There are times when what I does not fit into the "box" where it should assumedly fit. I have often wrestled with that.

I wrestled with being okay with who I was, although I always had a made-up mind not to be anyone else. I cared that the language I spoke may be different than others, but then again, not enough to speak a language that was not native to my experience. I've lived between two spectrums of identity until I understood that the best me was the one I was authentically called to be. I learned early to be that person and to resist the inner voices that attempted a buy-in to a model of confirming.

Our Lives Demonstrate Our Calling

During my formative years, I was unaware of all the doors, windows, and gates the enemy was attempting to use to destroy my spiritual inheritance and identity. On top of that, like many, I desired to do my own thing instead of obeying the principles established in my home. In my rebellion and desire to understand who I was and what was different about me, there was a turning point that caused me to journey toward God instead of away from him. This journey was necessary to comprehend what was different about me and how it was intended for the Kingdom of God, not the kingdom of darkness.

At this point, I had a limited understanding of my calling and my future, but the day came when I knew that God was calling me to do something that would tremendously impact the lives of others. Like most of us, we never fully understand the totality of what God requires of us until we start walking in His direction. Subsequently, we are unaware of the cost or the price we will pay for our "yes."

In retrospect, when I was young, my mom tried to best describe my calling as a leader and teacher. I would have school for the kids in my neighborhood and attempt to teach them things as though I was not their peer but one who was an apt tutor and mentor.

I wanted everyone to be informed, empowered, and on the same page. This started as early as kindergarten; when armed with an easel and chalk, I became an instructor, and they became students. I followed the precept for "no child left behind" before hearing the slogan. What I knew, I wanted them to know as well. Of course, it wasn't much more than they knew. However, I felt it was my obligation to mentor somehow, equip, train, and empower even back then.

The Things That Come To Inform And Shape Us

But as most of us know, "life" happens, and along with our youthful practices of attempting to become, there are also the things that serve to wound, injure, distract, and pull us off of God's path of formation within us. I veered and vacillated off that path as I dealt with insecurities, wounds, hurts, rejection, and the like. But inwardly, I maintained a sense of self that I knew later was beyond me and was God-given to uphold me through whatever life would present.

I developed a mantra of protection that taught me to be tough, strong, and on top of my game. I learned not to cry due to internal shaping occurring to what I believed at then to be for my good. I later realized this was my "go-to" protection mechanism. I didn't cry because I wanted to be tough, but instead, I wanted to be there for everyone else, crying. If we all were crying, who was "watching and helping."

In the end, this worked for my good to a degree. My desire to protect and defend others started early, and from that place, I developed the heart of a prayer warrior and intercessor. I relied on my inward gift to "perceive" and "know" but used it as a defense mechanism. In my rationale, I believed you could deal with whatever you saw if you could understand what's happening. I didn't understand that although discernment is powerful, it's not powerful enough to prevent you from wounds, hurt, or pain in every case. The foresight of injury is not enough to prevent us from participating in what will potentially harm us.

I Am Revival

I accepted Christ about thirty years ago, accepted my call twenty-five years ago, and realized quite a few years ago that a process is required to become who God called us to be. This process is deeper and more intensive in many cases than what we outline it to be as ministers in our sermons and lectures. This process is often a matter of life and death in being and becoming. At this point, I realize that far more than being a wife, a mother, prophet/pastor, counselor, and friend…I AM REVIVAL. I have endured a process of making, dismantling, rebuilding, tearing down, and restoration. I am shackled to a continual process of change and inward healing established to meet the mandate required by God.

This process spoke to how I related to church and my passion for change, revitalization, and renewal. I understood prayer early because I realized it was the primary spiritual discipline promoting change. If you need change, prayer is the avenue for it. Looking back over my life, I see how revival was always part of who I was and who I was becoming. I was never interested in the ordinary but always saw things through a lens that sometimes could be considered "uncommon." So much so that when my husband and I were clear about God leading us to plant a church, his voice confirmed the name, "Uncommon Church." This was what we saw, envisioned, embodied, and believed God was doing in our churches and everywhere. He was taking "ordinary people and preparing them to do uncommon things on the earth.

You Are Revival

Is this process unique to me? Not at all. I only share a small, minuscule part of my story as a point of identification. I sense that many others feel this way. Much of what has shaped and informed who I am today cannot be told in a chapter or this writing. However, one thing shared amongst those that ascribe to a kingdom mandate greater than themselves; is God's mark on their existence. They can look back over their life and see that every part of what God has allowed or disallowed has been necessary for becoming who He intended them to be from the beginning.

You may not be a prophet; however, the thought process remains the same as it did for Jeremiah when God confirmed this:

Jeremiah 1:5: "Before I formed you in the womb I knew you before you were born I set you apart; I appointed you as a prophet to the nations."

God created us with the privilege of a destined and determined end. He had good intentions toward us and prescribed a spiritual DNA code to our being that addresses our past, present, and future.

Jeremiah 29:11, "For I know the plans I have for you," declares the Lord, "plans to prosper you and not to harm you, plans to give you hope and a future."

This is the one reassurance to which "marked" men and women of God who are trailblazers, pioneers, agents of change, and revivalists can point back. That is where they realize that whatever they have experienced thus far was all part of the bigger picture and plan of God for their lives.

Without this "mark", many of us would have been like David and fainted unless we believed to see the salvation of the Lord in the land of the living. (Psalm 27:13-14)

He cares enough for His people that He does not want us to be fragmented but made whole. Revival is fueled by God's love. The engine of revival is God's continual process of transformation. This love toward us is so great that the Bible declares, "While we were yet sinners, Christ died for us" (Romans 5:8, NIV). His love requires us further, according to Romans 12:2;

> *"Do not conform to the pattern of this world, but be transformed by the renewing of your mind. Then you will be able to prove what God's will is--His good, pleasing and perfect will." (NIV)*

We Are Marked For Revival

My journey has not been easy, but my journey has acquainted me with the process of a deep inward change, and the love of God has renewed me. It has caused me to sincerely seek a Psalm 51:10 experience identified by the desire to have a clean heart and a right spirit. For those of you who have found yourself in the same place of transformation, follow me as I share some of the things I believe God uses to transform the lives of marked men or women, as they are being made to boldly promote revival and loudly proclaim, "I AM REVIVAL.

CHAPTER TWO

Revival 2.0: You Are An Agent Of Change

Revival Begins in the Individual's Heart. Let it Begin With You on Your Face Alone Before God. Turn From Every Sin That Might Hinder. Renew Yourself To A New Devotion to the Savior.

LEE ROBERSON

God is looking to use those willing to endure the process of heart transformation for this next move of God. Revival people are those who are willing to "do the work." They desire change but understand to facilitate "change," they must become "change."

That is the heart cry of the revivalist. If you believe that you have the God-given ability to change and shift; atmospheres, environments, and cultures for the kingdom of God, then you also are "REVIVAL." You carry the breath of revival, the winds of change in your being. When you experience revival within, you start desiring change as an inward work. Your life starts moving toward holiness, sanctification, purification, and righteousness. Essentially, your prayer becomes God make me more like you so that I can do and experience your will on earth.

Shift

There is a tremendous shifting of voices, perspectives, and ideas in our society and within the Body of Christ today. Now more than ever, we need people who are passionate about their stance as change agents and those willing to promote the agenda of Heaven on Earth. Within the body of Christ, every other agenda should be deemed irrelevant or secondary to the primary focus of representing Christ on Earth. In that regard, both men and women of God have been hidden in obscurity but are called forth in this hour, the finest hour in the history of the Church.

The existing crisis calls for a season of shifting, recalibration, and re-alignment. This adjustment speaks to a church that's not sleeping but willing to rise to the occasion. This level of awakening prompts revival both individually and internally but also prepares us to facilitate revival corporately and externally.

Revival is the shaking of systems, as well as deconstruction and reconstruction. But it requires a process, which most likely occurs when there appear to be times of drought and famine, both spiritually and naturally. In the midst of chaos, God focuses on rebuilding; not only His church but he grants us a new view of how things should be orchestrated. This, in turn, causes us to see the rise of new kingdom leaders with new mandates for ruling and reigning in authority and at the helm.

Haggai 2:6-9. says:

> *6 "This is what the Lord Almighty says: 'In a little while I will once more shake the heavens and the earth, the sea and the dry land. 7 I will shake all nations, and what is desired by all nations will come, and I will fill this house with glory,' says the Lord Almighty. 8 'The silver is mine and the gold is mine,'*

declares the Lord Almighty. 9 'The glory of this present house will be greater than the glory of the former house,' says the Lord Almighty. 'And in this place I will grant peace,' declares the Lord Almighty."

Also, in 2 Chronicles 7:14 (ASV), the scriptures say:

If my people, who are called by my name, shall humble themselves, and pray, and seek my face, and turn from their wicked ways; then will I hear from heaven, and will forgive their sin, and will heal their land.

We must come to grips with the fact that the shaking produced in this current season produced a turning over of systems, revealed dark truths and exposed gross darkness...

Isaiah 60:2 2 For, behold, the darkness shall cover the earth, and gross darkness the people: but the Lord shall arise upon thee, and his glory shall be seen upon thee."

But the Lord will arise in the midst of it all to reveal Himself and His people. We are the light carriers and the glory carriers that the world needs.

That process starts within to carry that level of glory back into the world. In turn, we will effectively be able to impact the Seven mountains of cultural influence; Religion, Family, Education, Government, Media, Arts & Entertainment, and Business.

Re-Present Christ

However, as the body of Christ, we live in a time when the church struggles with how we fit in a changing world. Everything is changing around us, and technology is ordering and structuring culture. While culture is being re-aligned in the world, some churches are looking for ways to acquiesce to culture, while others are busy ignoring it altogether.

Some will affirm changes in societal norms and culture. However, it will remain their responsibility to re-present the culture of the Kingdom. Due to the nature of shifting priorities and scattered identity within the church, this clarion call for change is louder now than before. It is time for the church to seek transformation, revival, and clear direction not to be influenced by the culture of the day but rather to become cultural influencers. A shift towards that end requires revival.

Revival Rising

When one considers the concept of revival, those familiar with the charismatic nuisances of the church will turn to scenes of wonderous glory, demonstration, and power amongst a gathering of God's people. However, with a closer look at revival, it benefits us to consider revival with an inward look, where we experience and encounter God in a way that turns our heart back to Him and produces people who are harvest-ready by way of restoration of the heart.

We have entered a season where it is clear from all aspects of prophetic proclamation that "revival" has come. This is the cry of the apostle, prophet, and many of God's people. In this cry, we must not lack the same cry for revival to start "in" us before we push for revival "for" us. This should not serve as a revelation because most of our references to revival in the scriptures require the posture of heart change preceding the manifestation of power or glory amongst the people of God.

At the core of revival are prayer and repentance. The impetus behind the movement or shift hinged upon prayer in every significant move of God or revival. Historically, we see the posture of men and women who desired change for their city, nation, region, etc., were also those who found themselves enduring tremendous seasons of prayer and travail. In that manner, those who carried the weight of revival also experienced the outcome of revival first within.

Revival Origins

> *In the beginning God created the heavens and the earth. 2 The earth was without form, and void; and darkness was on the face of the deep. And the Spirit of God was hovering over the face of the waters. Genesis 1:1-2*

From that place, God begins to speak to the earth and command the world to come out of a void place to a place of manifesting His original intent. The Spirit of God hovered over the waters and was the overseer for the manifestation of God's glory on earth. In the same manner, it is time for the church to again see the manifestation of the power of God on earth. However, it will require that we understand and re-visit the equipping ministry of power that the Holy Spirit possesses and provides.

For us to experience this next move of God, we must first realize His origins, His original intent, His personhood and not simply as an "it." We must acknowledge Him as the Spirit of Truth, God's divine power, and His ominscience. He is the Ruach: the very breath of God, the Pneuma; the wind of the Spirit.

Then we must understand His reason for coming in this manner:

> *John 15:26-27 "When the Counselor comes, whom I will send to you from the Father, the Spirit of truth who goes out from*

the Father, he will testify about me. 27 And you also must testify, for you have been with me from the beginning."

John 16:4-15: "I have told you this, so that when the time comes you will remember that I warned you. I did not tell you this at first because I was with you.⁵ "Now I am going to him who sent me, yet none of you asks me, 'Where are you going?' ⁶Because I have said these things, you are filled with grief. ⁷But I tell you the truth: It is for your good that I am going away. Unless I go away, the Counselor will not come to you; but if I go, I will send him to you. ⁸When he comes, he will convict the world of guilt[a] in regard to sin and righteousness and judgment: ⁹in regard to sin, because men do not believe in me; ¹⁰in regard to righteousness, because I am going to the Father, where you can see me no longer; ¹¹and in regard to judgment, because the prince of this world now stands condemned.¹² "I have much more to say to you, more than you can now bear. ¹³But when he, the Spirit of truth, comes, he will guide you into all truth. He will not speak on his own; he will speak only what he hears, and he will tell you what is yet to come. ¹⁴He will bring glory to me by taking from what is mine and making it known to you. ¹⁵All that belongs to the Father is mine. That is why I said the Spirit will take from what is mine and make it known to you."

At the point of your salvation you were sealed with the promise of the Holy Spirit. According to Ephesians 1:13;

In whom ye also trusted, after that ye heard the word of truth, the gospel of your salvation: in whom also after that ye believed, ye were sealed with that holy Spirit of promise,

The Holy Spirit is revealed in us as the paraclete; one called alongside, the counselor, one who encourages, and also as an intercessor. He is the one that is given to us as an equipper for the greater works that we are called to do.

He is our advocate, the one that searches the heart; the divine mind of God. He is the one that interprets our prayers and takes them to the Father. He hears and understands the very intimate moanings and groanings that we have.

The psalmist was so convinced of the work of the Holy Spirit that he said in Psalm 51:10;

Create in me a clean heart, O God, and renew a steadfast spirit within me. Do not cast me away from Your presence and do not take your Holy Spirit from me.

Then Paul follows with;

Romans 8:26 Likewise the Spirit also helpeth our infirmities: for we know not what we should pray for as we ought: but the Spirit itself maketh intercession for us with groanings which cannot be uttered.

With that in mind, we must understand that the SAME GOD was there doing the work of the HOLY SPIRIT in the EARLY CHURCH is the same GOD available to us now to do the work of ministry.

Acts 1:1-8: But you shall receive power when the Holy Spirit has come upon you; and you shall be witnesses to Me in Jerusalem, and in all Judea and Samaria, and to the end of the earth."

John 4:12 Very truly I tell you, whoever believes in me will do the works I have been doing, and they will do even greater things than these, because I am going to the Father.

1 Corinthian 2:9: Rather as is it written, "No eye has seen, no ear has heard, no heart has imagined, what God has prepared for those who love Him. 10 But God has revealed it to us by the Spirit. The Spirit searches all things, even the deep things of God.

He also convicts us of sin and righteousness, and reveals His will and the deep mysteries of God to us. He enables and empowers us to do the will of the Father and gives us gifts. He perfects, confirms, imparts to us, and assists us in our love walk.

Divine Move Of God

To that end, this is the season that the SPIRIT OF GOD is preparing the body for a divine move of GOD and we can expect to see the fulfillment of Acts 2:16-17:

*But this is what was spoken by the prophet Joel: against the brethren, Lord they were baptized in the name of the Lord Jesus speaking boldly in the, granting signs and wonders the Holy Spirit came upon them. And it shall come to pass in the last days, says God, That I will pour out of My Spirit on all flesh;Your sons and your daughters shall prophesy,
Your young men shall see visions, Your old men shall dream dreams.*

We have heard about or experienced the latter-day or more recent charismatic pentecostal revivals that shook nations, systems, and the church. However, God is ready to shake the kingdom of God again with the power of the Holy Ghost through us so that others outside of the four walls will experience Him. When revival comes to a specific place or location, I believe we will encounter people willing to allow every area of their life to be surrendered to the power of God in ways that go beyond our expectations, limitations, religious traditions, and notions.

This is a season where revival will hit the land, and it will be followed by a "Great Awakening." An awakening indicates that something has been in a state of deep sleep and slumber and must be informed of a need to rise to the occasion! Revival causes us to be informed not only of our need to come out of our slumber but also to inform the world to awaken to Christ. Ephesians 5:14 reminds us this way:

14 This is why it is said: "Wake up, sleeper, rise from the dead, and Christ will shine on you."

As the church arises, our role on the earth as the manifested sons of God will be revealed. There will become a greater urgency in this hour for not only believers but non-believers to experience miracles, signs, and wonders, and not because people are just interested in the supernatural, but because some of the situations are so severe that the only solution will be transformation by way of the miraculous.

We will start to see churches and homes become houses of prayer once again because there will be a greater need for "safe" spaces where believers and non-believers alike can go to be healed and delivered. In some churches, the presence of the Lord has been kicked out, so His inhabitation will be witnessed in spaces that are not considered "church" per se, but they are peculiar and unique spaces where people can experience the presence of God. Expect coffee houses, restaurants, movie theaters, and all types of uncommon spaces to be places where the presence of God will be hosted.

When the Lord pours out his spirit on all flesh, the way and the manner we've seen revival before will be different. Our revivals of the past focused on certain individuals, but in this season, revival will not be centralized in the same manner. We will begin to carry the anointing for revival in our lives, that whatever we are, the anointed to heal, set free and deliver will follow us. For those who yield to the miraculous, the miraculous will follow them.

God is dispensing out his glory so that we can distribute that same Glory on the earth. When you have come into real contact with the Glory of God and the Power of the Holy Spirit, you will not want to keep it to yourself. Instead, you will desire to become a distributor of it. When we come into contact with a good product, we most likely want to share that with others. For those who experience His glory in this hour, the desire will be to not keep it to yourself. Honestly, once you encounter God's glory in that manner, you cannot keep it to yourself.

The premise of this book is to ensure that we understand the necessity of being inwardly processed by revival while also expecting to experience revival corporately. As a result, we should expect revival to pop up all over the land without a presider, a worship team, and a flyer.

Yes, there will be worship, and yes, God will use individuals, but this is the day of the "all flesh" anointing, and the good thing is that while we are sitting in this midst of this latter-day church anointing, God is preparing a people for the most widespread occurrence of revival in the earth as He uses His people to become viable instances of revival everywhere they go. We've been given an assignment that requires us to be pointed back to Him, our first love, and His original intentions for us as the body of Christ. It all starts within.

A Turn Back To God

Acts 3:19-20 declares, "Repent therefore and be converted, that your sins may be blotted out, so that times of refreshing may come from the presence of the Lord, 20 and that He may send [a]Jesus Christ, who was [b]preached to you before," (NKJV)

Peter, in one of his most powerful sermons, provides us instructions for not only repentance but turning back to God. The concept of repentance in the Greek is to "metanoeō," to change one's mind. Changing one's mind is necessary; however proceeding change of mind, there should also be a "turn." The Greek word to turn back, "epistrephō" illustrates further a turn "back to" God."

While there has been a lull in revival language and the concept of revival in seasons past, it is the heart cry of the Father for His people to return to the true nature of revival. In this season, there is a call back to God like never before, where the people of God will desire to do whatever it takes to fulfill His kingdom mandates on the earth. This means that before we can get the spoils of the harvest, we must desire for God to destroy everything within us that separates us from being harvest-ready.

2 Chronicles 7:14 further demonstrates the intent of revival by declaring,

"If My people who are called by My name will humble themselves, and pray and seek My face, and turn from their wicked ways, then I will hear from heaven, and will forgive their sin and heal their land. (NKJV)

In that manner, prayer has always been the forerunner to revival, and the prayers of the saints spark the fire for revival. Revival will not be defined by a location but by people who desire increased access to the mind of God.

Ordinary People, Everyday Calling

This begs the question of what revival is. In that manner, the Body of Christ must be separated from the premise of revival being an established gathering of the saints for the sake of saying we "gathered."

The metric of success for revival must not be qualified by the mere fact that we prayed, fasted, had a great speaker, and our belief that those factors equate to "revival." Revival is not an occurrence of just visitation but rather the "continual presence" of God in an atmosphere, enviroment, or individual.

The spirit of the Lord comes upon us and prepares us to walk out our "every day" calling. God empowers us to be who He calls us to be daily not, only within the four walls of the church but outside of them as well.

If we reduce revival to a service only, we will surely miss the impact of living a transformed life. Now that you have cried, ran around the building, and rolled on the floor, what are you going to do with the revival fire that has been produced within?

Revival prompts the desire to move away from accommodating the normalcy of what we do as the church. The goal is that we step out into the realm of God's kingdom being demonstrated on earth through us. This is the diet of those who hunger and thirst for more of Him but also want to share God with others. These *"ordinary people"* have been uniquely qualified and marked as agents of change in others by the one who has called them to be a light in dark situations.

Revival is the recalibration, restoration, renewal, and re-installation of something that worked efficiently before but now requires a different method for proper functionality. When we experience revival within, we create a space in us and amongst us where God can continually dwell. The formula is simple for those who have committed themselves to a lifestyle of prayer and surrender. Revival-ready people who keep their ears to the hearts of God and their heart to the pulse of God.

Revival Uncovers Character Flaws

As a result, God deals with matters of the heart. Revival, in most cases, can be real "messy." Because things are being deconstructed, the process of reconstruction lends to an interesting process! Our character and integrity come under inspection, and what you work hardest to conceal is brought to the surface. This becomes a matter of identification of character flaws brewing in your life's backdrop. When our systems, methods, ideologies, theologies, and the like are being overturned and dealt with, we most likely don't want to run to that place of introspection but away from it.

Revival, in turn comes to expose and burn away what we desire to conceal and moves us towards what God wants to reveal in us. Revival is transformative, causing us to become who God desired us to be all along. It exposes the dark and grey areas of our life that have hindered our trajectory. His original intent for our lives is revealed through revival as we return to His original purpose.

Ultimately, the main propelling force of revival is God's love toward us and our ability to love ourselves and to extend the same love. We must love ourselves and others enough to desire change and demonstrate change. We often require love from others but are not willing to demonstrate that same type of love. So much of what we do in the name of love shows that we don't respect its power. Our intentions to gain love override our desire to give love in many situations. This type of love is not motivated by a heart that desires to sacrificially give love, which is the kind of love that Christ gave, but rather to only be loved.

Jesus is the best example of love, as He loved us even when we were not doing what He desired us to do. Yet, he still died for us. He wasn't concerned about whether we qualified for His love or had earned His love. His love was genuine, and full of grace and mercy. Love starts within and then pours out to others. Revival purifies our love walk and transforms our ability and capacity to be loved and to show love.

For God so loved the world, that He gave His only begotten Son, that whosoever believeth in Him should not perish, but have everlasting life. (John 3:16, KJV)

But God demonstrates His own love for us in this: While we are yet still sinners, Christ died for us.(Romans 5:8, KJV)

Love is the necessary fuel for the engine of revival.

The Revivalists Are Here

Our nations, cities, regions, territories, etc., can't be won for Christ if we remain the same. When we allow revival to work in us, we will become agents of change, and people will be drawn to what they now see of us. In that manner, revival will come upon you, to work in you, to flow through you, and to work out of you. You will become a change agent and glory carrier during this process.

Those around you will experience God's glory and the power of God when they encounter you. Simply put, when they encounter you they encounter Christ, the Hope of Glory, the

Way, the Truth, and the Life. When they encounter you, they ultimately encounter Him.

God is calling for the revivalist. The revivalists are the remnant saints aware of their ability to impact the lives of others via the mechanism of change. They are willing to be changed to facilitate change. Revivalists are willing to employ the inner workings of the Holy Spirit to refine and perfect them. He's perfecting everything concerning us for his pleasure and for the sake of his people experiencing the full quality of life that He intended for his people from the beginning.

The desire for revival is brewing not only within me but others in the body of Christ. Revival has always excited, fascinated, and sparked a fire within me. The thought of the revivalists and revival movements of days gone by absolutely amaze me. However, some attributes and character traits are necessary for those desiring to become bold, daring ambassadors for change and revival on the earth. Hence, we avoid repeating mistakes that hindered past revivals.

The reformers of this hour don't look like what we told ourselves they should look like in seasons past. This will be difficult to deal with for some. There is a rising remnant that may not fit our standards or the ones the church has established. If you don't fit the model, be okay with it because the remnant that's rising is coming with power! They will shake systems, shift paradigms, and dismantle the kingdom of darkness by exhibiting the kingdom of light on Earth!

Hopefully, this book will admonish you as the reader to consider areas of your life where God is shifting you to walk in the fullness of faith and purpose towards inward change, brokenness, and surrender. In turn, this stance will produce everyday occurrences of revival, changing you within, and working through you to be a glory carrier and revivalist on earth.

CHAPTER THREE

Recalibration: Divine Alignment

> *In revival, God is not concerned about filling empty churches, He is concerned about filling empty hearts.*
>
> LEONARD RAVENHILL

The Body of Christ is being recalibrated in this hour so that we can align with God's original intent for His church. I believe there is a glory reserved for the latter house that we've yet to see, but God is ready to reveal it. For the manifestation of glory and demonstration of God's power to be revealed, He will recalibrate His people and restore them to a place conducive to revival.

The Necessity Of Recalibration

To RECALIBRATE means, basically to CALIBRATE AGAIN.

Calibrate: to adjust precisely for a particular function; to measure precisely, especially against a standard (**merriam-webster.com**).

Recalibrate: to calibrate something again or differently. (**google.ca**). To make small changes to an instrument so that it measures accurately; to change the way you do or think about something (dictionary.cambridge.org).

God has a specific purpose, destiny, and calling on your life. When you were created, it was not without purpose or reason. He's looking to demonstrate His character and nature on the earth through His people. Revivalists are often confronted with the vast chasm between the person the enemy is trying to identify them as and the one they are called to be.

When you are called to effect change, the greatest struggle experienced is based on the purpose of God in your life and the reason you were born. The quicker you work on agreeing with God about who he says you are, the closer you get to experience more of Christ's operation in your life.

For we are His workmanship, created in Christ Jesus for good works, which God prepared beforehand so that we would walk in them. (Ephesians 2:10, NKJV)

For I know the thoughts that I think toward you, says the Lord, thoughts of peace and not of evil, to give you a future and a hope. (Jeremiah 29:11, NKJV)

To them God willed to make known what are the riches of the glory of this mystery among the Gentiles: which is Christ in you, the hope of glory. (Colossians 1:27, NKJV)

God is shaking out of place the things that don't align with his will, purpose, and plan, and he is putting into place the things that do. One of the primary functions of revival is the restoration of the heart, soul, and will of man. However, we often see believers are functioning in a place where deliverance is necessary. Self-examination and self-evaluation will help us to identify the areas in our lives that are not under God's control and governance but actually under the control of our flesh. We have to take spiritual responsibility for our own lives. We can't wait around like the man by the pool for someone to come and deliver us (John 5:15).

When you notice something is off in your life, that is the time to position yourself for your freedom and deliverance. But to be set free, you must identify what is holding you back. Further, you must know that you have been granted authority to be free. Many of us are not free because we don't believe we can be set free. We are waiting for our pastors, leaders, or favorite minister to lay hands on us and "set us free." The truth is the deliverance we desire starts within. Deliverance requires we know what needs to be changed and start that conversation of change within and with the Father. Yes, He will use others to assist us in the journey, but those individuals are limited to the "surrender" required to facilitate change.

Essentially, the adage remains true "I can take you to the water, but I can't make you drink." The choice to drink from the everlasting fountain of life found in Jesus is a choice that we must make. The story of the Samaritan women at the well is full of the heart cry of Jesus for reformation and inward change. He represents deliverance before her as he offers himself as an agent of change in her situation. John 4:7-15 reads:

"7 When a Samaritan woman came to draw water, Jesus said to her, "Will you give me a drink?" 8(His disciples had gone into the town to buy food.) 9The Samaritan woman said to him, "You are a Jew and I am a Samaritan woman. How can you ask me for a drink?" (For Jews do not associate with Samaritans.[a]) 10Jesus answered her, "If you knew the gift of God and who it is that asks you for a drink, you would have asked him and he would have given you living water." 11"Sir," the woman said, "you have nothing to draw with and the

well is deep. Where can you get this living water? 12Are you greater than our father Jacob, who gave us the well and drank from it himself, as did also his sons and his flocks and herds?" 13Jesus answered, "Everyone who drinks this water will be thirsty again, 14but whoever drinks the water I give him will never thirst. Indeed, the water I give him will become in him a spring of water welling up to eternal life." 15The woman said to him, "Sir, give me this water so that I won't get thirsty and have to keep coming here to draw water." (NIV)

God desires to quench the thirst of those who desire change. Jesus acknowledges the Samaritan women's issue of having multiple husbands in order to inform her of the reality that she requires deliverance. What she needed, He had. She was thirsty, but He had the thirst quencher. He desires to give you something that will cause you to change and experience transformation in every aspect of your life. He wants you to drink of Him so that you will be like the Samaritan woman in the end, who said, "Come, see a man that told me all I ever did." Even though He knew everything I did, He loved me enough to help, save, and give me life-changing power. While this is His desire, it must become ours as well to be set free from everything that would attempt to entangle and ensnare us.

The thief does not come except to steal, and to kill, and to destroy. I have come that they may have life, and that they may have it more abundantly. (John 10:10 NKJV)

Blessed are those who hunger and thirst for righteousness, For they shall be filled. (Matthew 5:6, NKJV)

We have been given the authority to bind and loose. Matthew 18:18 tells us, "Assuredly, I say to you, whatever you bind on earth will be bound in heaven, and whatever you loose on earth will be loosed in heaven." Many of us can't synchronize with heaven because we are bound on earth by our flesh. We are bound by our inability to mature in Christ.

We have not sought the deliverance we need. We are more connected to our flesh than our spirit, and in many cases, this keeps us connected to the yoke of bondage that restrains us from being free. Many of us are not experiencing heaven on earth because we have not denounced hell within. We need to be freed up to assist God in freeing others.

Matthew 7:5 says, "Hypocrite, first remove the plank from your own eye, and then you will see clearly to remove the speck from your brother's eye." (NKJV)

The sin in our lives doesn't remove God from our lives, but will result in broken fellowship. If we seek to draw closer to God, we can't remain the same. When we allow revival to work in us, we will be more equipped to facilitate change in others. People literally will be drawn to what they now see of us. When they realize that change has occured, they will want to know more about the change they see in us.

A major construct of revival "within" is drawing closer to God. Drawing closer to Him means something will change, and what changes will produce revival. To repeat the same formula, this level of change comes upon you, works in you, flows through you, and works out of you. It will produce fire, power, and unearthed potential in you! We are not drawing closer to God just for ourselves but so that the kingdom of GOD can advance. That means that as you become a change agent and glory carrier, the people around you will begin to experience the Glory and indwelling of the presence of the Lord. Simply put, when they encounter you, they encounter Christ, the hope of Glory, the way, the truth, and the life.

We have been given dominion authority on earth, and we should pursue domination in every area by advancing the kingdom of God and dismantling the kingdom of darkness. Our desire should be to pursue in this manner until we see the narrative of Revelation 11:15 fulfilled: "The kingdoms of the world now belong to our Lord and his Anointed, and he will reign forever and ever." (NASB)

Revival Shifts Old Paradigms

In that manner, revival is not just this event where thousands of people show up in one location for a couple of months to a year either. In this hour, revival will not just be what happens on Sunday or during the week but what happens every day as we experience the supernatural move of God daily in action and demonstration. When we see revival as an everyday construct, revival will happen whenever we gather.

The atmosphere will be revival ready. There are churches that will always be in revival mode. Their membership may be transient because God will use them as training centers and houses of worship and prayer. People will come in, receive the equipping and training they need and go out to other assignments to do the work they have been called to do. When people gather in these "marked" locations, people will encounter the presence of God. This presence will not only tickle their emotions but accelerate their destiny.

This will be the model that establishes that we are not just gathering weekly to do church, but we become the church. It's the model that exists to demonstrate a people who no longer focuses on the pastor doing all the work but the five-fold ministry and the people of God working together to accomplish ministry. It will be the model where church is not just for eating and swallowing a good message but also prompts us to re-produce what we've been fed. This model produces people who speak words that are spirit and life and delivers outcomes that transform lives. Remember, Paul says it like this in; delivers outcomes that transform lives. Remember Paul, says it like this in:

> *1 Corinthians 2:1-6 "And I, brethren, when I came to you, did not come with excellence of speech or of wisdom declaring to you the [a]testimony of God. 2 For I determined not to know anything among you except Jesus Christ and Him crucified. 3 I was with you in weakness, in fear, and in much trembling. 4 And my speech and my preaching were not with persuasive words of [b]human wisdom, but in demonstration of the Spirit and of power, 5 that your faith should not be in the wisdom of men but in the power of God." (NKJV)*

When revival comes on a people, God opens their hearts to desire change and to be closer to Him. Revival must be written on the tablets of our hearts. Revival is built into the core of our spiritual DNA when we desire to be agents of change, and it outflows from us as the expression of transformation that occurs from within. When we desire to be closer to God, it is a revival statement in and of itself.

There is a sound that is associated with revival. Transformation carries a sound, a volume, a weight of glory and light. There are those that carry a distinct sound that God will use to express revival on the earth. Yes, it may be in songs or a particular message or word, but that is not the only way. The "sound" He will use will go out into the earth and signify to others that revival has come. Some carry the sound of "revival" within, as evidenced in how they demonstrate, articulate, and show up in every space they show up in.

They shift rooms, atmospheres, spaces, places, people, entities, etc. They are "glory carriers" whose sound has been given as a gift to transform everything they encounter. They have history with God, and when you leave their presence, you know they have been in His presence. Their lives are transformative, potent, and full of God's glory, and their sound carries the weight of revival! The sound is in their being, upon them, and moves through them! The sound they carry will produce and open portals of heavens in rooms and spaces where believers gather. However, it will also produce transformation just in simple conversations and by encountering those who carry the distinct nature of revival.

There Is A Move Closer Toward God

How do we become closer to God? We do so by accessing the supernatural model of revival and by the power of prayer and spending time in the presence of GOD. Ezekiel's experience in the Valley of Dry Bones helps us by depicting an illustration for revival. The word of God expressed in Ezekiel 37:1-3:

> *"The hand of the Lord came upon me and brought me out in the Spirit of the Lord, and set me down in the midst of the valley; and it was full of bones. 2 Then He caused me to pass by them all around, and behold, there were very many in the open valley; and indeed they were very dry. 3 And He said to me, "Son of man, can these bones live?" (NKJV)*

When God gets ready to put flesh on bones, He revives a people and causes a new structure from the "ineffective prior model." He recalibrates the bones, puts new flesh on them, and then commands the bones to move. But to align with God, we must move into a new place of prayer and time spent in his presence.

Prayer is the catalyst for change. That is the main reason why we pray. We pray because we need God to change something in our current situation and circumstance. 90% of our prayers express a need for something to be different, changed, fixed, and restored. First, we must be willing to acknowledge our need to pray differently. We need a different paradigm regarding prayer, a different strategy.

In the biblical narrative, Ezekiel responds to God's question regarding whether dry bones can live this way, "So I answered, "O Lord God, you know." He acknowledges his situation and fully understands there is something wrong. Something is not working correctly here. This improper functionality requires a move, a shift. There must be an adjustment for something to go from death to life. The Lord asked can these bones live, and surely, they can. However, that will require supernatural modifications.

This ultimately means we can't deal with old wineskins. What happens is that God works on a continuum of shifting paradigms. He is a God of restoration and revolution. He takes what exists in one form and supernaturally causes it to exist in another form.

In the "Valley of Dry Bones," we see God is dealing with bones that were operating in one way, and then He allows them to be scattered and disconnected. Death occurred because something living was no longer functioning as it should. God then pronounces to Ezekiel that he has a supernatural ability to speak to dry bones and cause them to live.

We have to speak to the old structures for a new structure to arise again in the church. We have been granted the power to decree and prophesy to failed structures, new purpose, intent, new functions, new paradigms, and new ways of thinking, living, moving, and being. We will not be able to put new wine in old wineskins. Matthew 9:16-17:

No one puts a piece of unshrunk cloth on an old garment;

for [a]the patch pulls away from the garment, and the tear is made worse. Nor do they put new wine into old wineskins, or else the wineskins [b]break, the wine is spilled, and the wineskins are ruined. But they put new wine into new wineskins, and both are preserved." (NKJV)

Then he said to me, "Prophesy to these bones and say to them, 'Dry bones, hear the word of the Lord! 5 This is what the Sovereign Lord says to these bones: I will make breath[a] enter you, and you will come to life. 6 I will attach tendons to you and make flesh come upon you and cover you with skin; I will put breath in you, and you will come to life. Then you will know that I am the Lord." (NIV) Ezekiel 37:4-6

Upon Ezekiel's revelation, and as he accesses knowledge from on high, he receives a simple command from God, to "prophesy". God tells him this is what I am about to do…I am prepared to make dry bones live again. When God pronounces life to a dead situation, it is time to time to get on board with His plan. His plan is to revive the dead places, dead areas, dead churches, dead people, and dead entities. Our only choice is to agree and work the plan until we see what God envisions come forth.

Ezekiel 37:9-10: Then he said to me, "Prophesy to the breath; prophesy, son of man, and say to it, 'This is what the Sovereign Lord says: Come, breath, from the four winds and breathe into these slain, that they may live.'" So I prophesied as he commanded me, and breath entered them; they came to life and stood up on their feet—a vast army. (NIV)

Instructions have been given, and God says to "prophesy." We are in the position to speak what He commands. We do this in prayer. Ezekiel is instructed to prophesy to the four winds (the whole earth), which means "nobody" is excluded. God wants to touch the world. In order to touch the world, God requires an army. The next illustration is that the bones stood on their feet, and a new structure arose as a great army.

God is looking for a great army of intercessors and people willing to take up the mandate of new structures on the earth. Revivalists are those willing to think outside the box and look for new ways of hosting God's glory on earth. They are called to the seven cultural mountains of family, religion, education, media, entertainment, business, and government, as we are empowered to influence them. God is not just drawing us closer to Him so we can be more spiritual or knowledgeable. He is drawing us closer because He is requiring more of us. He is looking for people who will take up their calling and move forward in his purpose. He is especially calling people in this hour back to a place of prayer. What is the end result of you drawing closer to Him? It has to be more than getting more of Him for ourselves. The end goal must become more of Him in us so that more of Him can be dispensed in the earth through us.

Alongside people who will pray and fulfill the call to be more intimate in their relationship with Christ via the vehicle of prayer, we also need the prophetic anointing of the watchman.

> *"I have posted watchmen on your walls, O Jerusalem; they will never be silent day or night. You who call on the LORD, give yourselves no rest, and give him no rest till he establishes Jerusalem and makes her the praise of the earth." (Isaiah 62:6-7, NIV)*

In drawing closer to God, we must also expect to become hosts of the presence of the Lord. Revival requires not only people who will seek the face and God and repent but also skilled intercessors. There's a clarion call for intercessors who sense an urgency to pray and tap into deeper dimensions and realms of prayer.

As they do so, there are portals in the heavens made accessible as they petition the courts of heaven on behalf of others. These intercessors will also gain stronger levels of prophetic sensitivity and power. Intercessors at this stage will know their role, understand their function, and boldly operate in their calling. Their kingdom assignment will mandate purity of heart in spiritual matters and proper motivation for ministry.

God is purifying the vessels and pouring oil into vessels that are not looking to make their name known but rather to make the name of Jesus famous. He is looking for those who desire the power of God to be established on the earth until the kingdoms of the world have become the kingdoms of our Lord and of His Christ. When Hezekiah prayed, his motivation in prayer was not that people would be saved and he would become the hero for praying such a great prayer, but instead, He says in Isaiah 37:20, "Now therefore, O Lord our God, save us from his hand, that all the kingdoms of the earth may know that You are the Lord, You alone." (NKJV)

Not only are the watchmen being prepared, but the prophets. He is purifying the prophetic dimension and those that will give language to revival and carry specific instructions to those who are mantled for revival. Prophets not only carry the word of wisdom, word of knowledge, prophetic utterances, and intercession, but they carry blueprints, strategies, solutions, and patterns in their being. They are given to assist, strengthen, and undergird apostolic movements and shifting paradigms. When utilized properly, they benefit those that will receive them

This is the season that God assigns prophets to specific and distinct missions. Those who have stood the test of time, been processed properly and thoroughly, and obtained weight and depth to their mantle/mandate you have been assigned!

Some people will request your assistance in building, plowing, and developing what God has given them! Be ready for this next move because revival is necessary for prophets and prophetic people to go forth, as well as new wineskins for apostolic leadership.

Purified Hearts

Revival comes to purify our hearts and bring us to a place of self-examination. Often, we have allowed an entry point into our lives where deception becomes so deep-rooted that it takes sincere excavation to get to the "root" of the issue. In that instance, we have mastered the art of covering up our sins instead of submitting our hearts to God so He can expose the areas that require purification.

> *Psalm 51:10 Create in me a clean heart, O God; and renew a right spirit within me.*

As the church is being recalibrated, the guard is changing. We have said it for years, but there is a shifting of sounds and voices in the earth that will carry the church into this new move. These will lead us to reformation, reinvention, and restructuring the church. Some are still hidden in obscurity because they will seemingly come out of nowhere when God releases them. However, they were in the fiery process of being made for this moment. They have endured the process.

So that means we have to be prepared to be processed. Our hearts are being refined, purified, and cleansed. I've seen how God is taking so many as if it was a course or class. Many of us have received several degrees during fiery trials and processes. Are you familiar with the place where every area of your life has seemingly been tested for purity? How do you deal with an offense? How do you process pain? How do you manage betrayal? How do you deal with rejection? I have seen God show me where I failed royally in every area.

My response to this level of introspection had to be to pray and work more than I ever had to be healed/delivered. I had to identify some things I could not allow in my ear gate. I know who does and doesn't have the capacity for me. I'm learning who I can and can not receive from, and none of this is not about being prideful but just knowing; what to regard and what not to regard. And a lot of it has been painful.

But in this hour, if you want to carry His glory; you will need to become okay with being closely associated with pain; the pain of familiarity, rejection, past wounds, etc. To get what God has next for you, learn His response to it all. For many of us, God is about to shoot us to our next dimension, but to do so, He had to pull us back into Him so that when we go forth, He can thrust us further than we were before.

For many of us, we've been looking for certain endorsements and people to validate us, and we could not figure out why that never happened. And the answer is simple...what God wants to do in us is not by way of our natural process of elevation and promotion. According to Psalm 75:6-7:

For promotion cometh neither from the east, nor from the west, nor from the south. But God is the judge: he putteth down one, and setteth up another.

God determines who He will set up and who He will put down. All of this is not about us. It's all bout Him and His kingdom being advanced. The word kingdom, (basilea) in the Greek language describes the sphere of God's rule. It speaks to the order of the King, His way of doing and being, His government and its operation. According to Psalms 22:8;

For the kingdom is the LORD'S: and he is the governor among the nations.

There's a process, a process specifically designed for those who are intended to come front and center in advancing the kingdom. And this process definitely has death attached to it. Paul says in I Corinthians 15:31; "I die daily", echoes Jesus' command to those who want to follow Him: "If anyone would come after me let him deny himself, take up his cross daily, and follow me" (Luke 9:23). For us to reign with Him, we will have to suffer…The good news is that although the Bible says….

2 Timothy 2:12: If we suffer, we shall also reign with him: if we deny him, he also will deny us:

The Good News is:

1 Peter 5:10: *And the God of all grace, who called you to his eternal glory in Christ, after you have suffered a little while, will himself restore you and make you strong, firm and steadfast.*

Romans 8:10: *I consider that our present sufferings are not worth comparing with the glory that will be revealed in us.*

Psalms 34:19: *Many are the afflictions of the righteous, but the Lord delivers him from them all.*

However, this process is not devoid of pain. The absence of pain may very well be the absence of purpose. Purpose requires pain because pain indicates what needs attention and needs to be healed. God presented you with pain so that you could be cognizant and aware of what He needs to restore within you in order to get "out" of you what he desires!

The Holy Spirit is the most powerful agent of change and transformative power available to us. One of the symbols of the Holy Spirit is fire, which is associated with purification. Fire also is used to identify with God's anger and judgment on one hand, and on the other, the approval and presence of God. We love it when the "fire of God" shows up to favor us. We love it when the "fire" assists us in having a "powerful service." But when He shows up to light a match under us, the story changes, as we don't like that type of fire as much.

When we consider what fire comes to do in our lives today, it is most symbolic of the Holy Spirit as a purifying agent. The Holy Spirit is the master agent of change. The Holy Spirit abides within the believer and serves as a "housekeeper." He desires to cleanse our spiritual house. He removes the "dross" or the worthless rubbish from our life.

In Easton's bible dictionary, Dross is defined as "the impurities of silver separated from one in the process of melting." When revival comes, it's as if God is melting or molding us into His Image. That process requires the "worthless rubbish" within us to come to the surface as the master refiner removes everything seen as an impurity. Hebrews 12:29 states, "For our God is a consuming fire." Let's seek to be revived instead of being deceived by our hearts! The things that are purified in the fire produces pure gold, but that which is covered up will only smother us.

The activation of the Holy Spirit, the fire of God, and the wind of revival upon you will cause you to be able to impact nations! According to Isaiah 1:25-26 (NIV) and Zechariah 13:9 (NIV):Isaiah 1:25-26:
"I will turn my hand against you;
I will thoroughly purge away your dross

and remove all your impurities.
I will restore your leaders as in days of old,
your rulers as at the beginning.
Afterward, you will be called
the City of Righteousness,
the Faithful City."
Zechariah 13:9
This third I will put into the fire;
I will refine them like silver
and test them like gold
They will call on my name
and I will answer them;
I will say, "They are my people,
and they will say, "The Lord is our God."

This fire that has come upon you came not only to purify you but to empower you. Once you have endured the fire, you will come out as pure gold! The refiner's fire will have produced what it intended to produce.

You will be one that may appear drunk, but the fire and power of God are setting you up to demonstrate His glory.

This is the season that God will use His fire to birth you, to propel you, and to invest His glory in you!

This fire is not sent to destroy you but to perfect you for your expected end!

This fire will open doors and initiate everything God has ordained for your life.

This fire will cause you to rise out of the ashes of despair, depression, and Lodabar!

This fire has come to confirm who you were all along and

press you into your next!

This fire will cause you to dream again, speak again, see again, and live again.

This fire will cause your family to be saved, your co-workers to be delivered, and your children to walk in their calling!

This fire is about to make policy, laws, and regulations change in your city, country, and the world!

God is burning some things off you to burn His impression in you!

Revival has come to expose the issues within the body of Christ at large and the things that require purification within. God's next move will challenge believers to grow, mature, and be changed as we become the "bride of Christ" that Jesus is returning for. Essentially, God is taking you "back to the future." As revivalists, we have to deal with both dimensions of the past and the future.

God will cause you to re-visit your past and deal with everything that exists there so that He can catapult you into your future. How you navigate the future will be contingent on how well you deal with the past. This is a must. You can not get around dealing with the trauma, hurt, or pain of the past. You owe your future to show up as your best self. To carry His glory, the weight of the past must go so that you will not be locked out of the glory that shall be revealed in and through you in the future.

While here, God requires a tremendous work of transformation that will impact us not only individually as believers but also corporately as the Body of Christ. As we shift in this direction, the power and ability of the church to attract the unchurched will again increase. We will see the reinstitution of the Five-Fold ministry operating as it should, and everyone will be in place to become the "Church" that Jesus died for. This act of revival will require RECALIBRATION!

In the last days, God says, I will pour out my Spirit on all people. Your sons and daughters will prophesy, your young men will see visions and your old men will dream dreams. Even on my servants, both men and women, I will pour out my Spirit in those days, and they will prophesy . (Acts 2:17-18)

The Heavens are open, and revival has come! As we experience revival within ourselves and then experience the manifest presence of God and glory encounters, we will see the Holy Spirit being poured on all men!

Recalibration Prayer:

- I turn away from the areas of sin and unrepentant places in my life that I have not allowed to be touched by the cleansing power of God. Mt.4;17, Acts 3:19, Acts 20:21
- I decree that my mind is strengthened and fortified today and God reveals every area where I have not allowed the yoke destroying anointing and power of God to dismantle every issue, weight, chain, fetter, and proclivity of my flesh. Psalm 139:23, Psalms 51:10-13, Isaiah 10:27
- ***Recalibrate me!*** Align me to your will, your purposes, and plan for my life. Psalm 143:10
- There is nothing that I will allow to separate me from fully engaging God in spirit and truth. I desire for my life to be pleasing to you Lord. John 4:24
- Show me the areas in my life that I have not

surrendered to you and allow your divine governance to overthrow every place that I have not surrendered. Romans 12:12, Galatians 2:20, Luke 9:23-24
- I align my mind, soul, spirit and body to be an offering unto you Lord, as I desire to serve you in manner that is pleasing. 1 Thessalonians 5:23
- I remind myself today that I am seated in heavenly places, and I take my rightful position now as I fully walk in the full armor of God. Ephesians 2:6-7, Ephesians 6:10
- I wrestle not against flesh and blood but against evil forces, the rulers, authorities, and powers of the kingdom of darkness and spiritual forces of evil in the heavenly realms. Ephesians 6:12-13
- I put on the full armor of God according to Ephesians 6:10-18 with the belt of truth and the breastplate of righteousness that solidifies my standing as I move towards becoming the uncompromisingly righteous and my belief that the just shall live by faith.
- My feet are ready to carry the gospel of peace today...
- I take up the shield of faith, so that I may extinguish all the fiery darts of the enemy.
- The Helmet of Salvation is placed upon my head and I gather the Sword of the Spirit, which is the word of God as I release his word over my life.
- The spirit of disunity and dishonor is broken in my life today.
- The spirit of sabotage, contention, and dissension is dismantled and has no power of authority over me.
- I believe my life will stand to exhibit the miraculous power of God in demonstration and with power. 1 Corinthians 2:4
- I believe you for a greater manifestation of glory, power, and presence in my life daily.
- I believe that the heavens are now open heavens and from them comes sustainable increase, wealth,

- streams of blessing, favor, healing, and glory! Philippians 4:19, Psalm 5:12, Psalm 90:17, Psalm 106:4, 2 Corinthians 9:8
- The Law of reciprocity and favor works continually and in full operation in my life. Luke 6:38
- I wholeheartedly agree that miracles, signs, and wonders shall be performed in and through me by the divine assistance of Holy Spirit. Hebrews 2:4, Romans 15:18-19, Ephesians 3:20-21, Acts 19:11-12, Mark 16:17-20
- The anointing to breakthrough is made available to me now and every spirit that would attempt to prevent breakthrough is brought under the subjection of the power of God. Isaiah 60:1-22, Acts 1:8, Micah 2:13, 2 Samuel 5:20
- You are bringing me around the right company of people and after being in their presence I will leave their presence as a changed man. 1 Samuel 10
- The blood of Jesus covers and seals today. Hebrews 9:14, 1 John 1:7, Matthew 26:28,
- The power of God is given full reign to heal, set free and deliver in any area in my life where healing, freedom, and deliverance is required. Hebrews 1:3, Colossians 2:12, Romans 15:13, Ephesians 3:20, 2 Timothy 1:7, 2 Peter 1:3
- There is an uncommon anointing available to me today.
- I decree and declare Uncommon Favor, Uncommon Supply, Uncommon Riches, Uncommon Success, and an Uncommon Anointing!

CHAPTER FOUR

"The Call To Live"

As long as we are content to live without revival, we will.

LEONARD RAVENHILL

A revivalist becomes acquainted with the necessity of identity as they endeavor to fulfill the will of God in their lives. One of the greatest crises in the body of Christ today is a lack of personal and individual identity. Without a correct understanding of something, we tend to undervalue it or appropriately ascribe honor to "it."

Identity Crisis Can Cause A State Of Emergency

Many of us have resorted to a place of slow death. We have been through so much pain, disappointment, and hurt that it has pulled us away from the original intent or purpose for our existence. We have seemingly been through situation after situation, trial upon trial, and devastation after devastation, and without proper re-fueling (prayer, faith, counsel), it's easy for us to exist in a state of emergency due to identity crisis.

A state of emergency means something is at stake or a sudden acute crisis appears. Political, economic, natural, and spiritual states of emergency may occur. However, nothing is more detrimental to the soul of an individual than a state of emergency or crisis that happens within. The truth is that many of us have been in crisis mode for so long that we are far from being acquainted with how we arrived there or with the root cause. However, there was an incident or something that happened, which now informs us that we are in a state of emergency in our personal lives.

When God is working revival within His people, He will alert us to the necessity of transformation, often through the means of emergency. Our senses can become so dull that we live in a manner that consists of going through the motions without cognition. We are unaware of the need for transition until the emergency occurs. The root word of "emergency" is emergence- which means to arise, to come to a place of understanding and change. When there is an emergency, there should be an emergence, a place of arising to the occasion, because a shift is now inevitable.

Maybe it was the doctor's report, the loss of a job, the loss of a relationship, the death of someone we loved, etc., that now requires revision due to our status change. However, the emergency informs something within and requires a shift in our stance, posture, and position to be made urgently. I have endured several occurrences that I knew were personal states of emergency. Whether financial, physical, or relational, I learned that one of the keys to surviving the emergency was first to acknowledge something in the situation that could be used to develop me further.

The clarion call and mandate for authenticity have grown stronger due to the existing identity crisis. The desire to return to who we are at the core is more important now than ever. The necessity of this return is even more vital in the body of Christ since we are brought with a price, blood-washed believers, the called out, set apart ekklesia that have the mandate to look like and express the image of Christ in the earth, simply put we are on assignment.

God is looking for kingdom citizens who will be okay with who they are and who they are not. They will not fight to pull the church into a model or stance below the standard of who God called them to be. They will not conform, nor will they compromise. Once you have been through what seems like consistent warfare and now come to the understanding that there was a reason the enemy has been fighting you so hard, you only have one choice: to decide to become the very thing he attempted to destroy. Your purpose is a threat to his kingdom, and coming out of agreement with him about the "real you" stands to be the thing that has him shaking in his boots! So let every state of emergency inform you of who you are becoming.

In addition, while we should be in an age of Renaissance, the church has seemingly been between states of being unconscious and drunk. We have gotten so drunk off everything that it should not matter. It is as though we've taken a tremendously long nap. We've been so drunk off of ourselves that we were gently lulled into sleep by the enemy, resulting in a lack of sobriety.

So, while we have slept through divine moments meant to align us, revive and restore us to the original intent of what the church should be, we've looked toward the moves of God of the past and waited for them to be reinstated when we should've been looking for a current move. Azusa was great, but what is God doing now? We expect to see God move in this present age with a present move!

While honoring the past, we must secure our future and utilize the relevant solutions for our day. We have a problem, and that problem remains. We are still determining how to reach the masses, but there is an answer. God is making you the solution to a problem that currently exists. Just as the songwriter says:

How to reach the masses, *men of ev'ry birth,
For an answer Jesus gave the key:
"And I, if I be lifted up from the earth,
Will draw all men unto Me."

Does your life lift him to the point that he has no other choice to respond and draw all men unto Him?

Wake Up!

While in this unconscious and drunken state, we were concerned about everything that concerned us and not much about what concerned God. However, in this season, God calls us back to sobriety. He calls us to the place where we are alert and not paralyzed by our drunkenness and spiritual stupor. When people are under the influence of a slumbering spirit, they're not awakened to the things of God. They are unable to pray consistently or to worship with the fervor and zeal that God desires.

So God is calling us to arise, to awaken.....according to Romans 13:11, "And do this, understanding the present time. The hour has come for you to wake up from your slumber because our salvation is nearer now than when we first believed." We can no longer let the issues of the day cause us to be paralyzed, sleep, drunk or comatose...we must awaken.

When Life Happens

I know what it feels like to be in a paralyzed state and to feel like the walking dead because of my situation. My husband and I have endured several storms together, primarily because we have worked to keep the things happening outside (externally) from coming inside (into our marriage). The external things were the typical list of trials that we all deal with family, finances, sickness, relationship issues, etc. When we encountered bankruptcy, this was not a matter of fault for either spouse. It was a matter of job loss and health issues occurring simultaneously. When we resolved to file for bankruptcy, we had never missed a house payment, car payment, etc., before. However, we knew we could not recover our financial picture once job loss and sickness hit us simultaneously.

The lesson we learned was what appeared to be total destruction was the foundation for restoration within us. When we are endearing storms, we often resort to guilt, shame, and looking for a way to blame someone for what's happening to us. If we can only get to the root cause of the issue and see what's going on, be it warfare, a matter of poor decisions, or simply "life happening," we'll be better able to overcome and maintain relationships, dignity, and our sanity at the end of the ordeal. Situations that look like the death of you can be used tremendously to birth depth of character in you when you allow it.

We must remain more mindful of the life available to us than what appears to be the death that surrounds us in our crisis moments. Revivalists will stare death in the eye and believe for the best out of the worst situations because they realize their ability to overcome is necessary for purpose to be fulfilled. Ezekiel 16:6 shares, *"Then I passed by and saw you kicking about in your blood, and as you lay there in your blood, I said to you, "Live!"* (NIV) The people's state of emergency necessitated the voice of God to command life in a dead situation.

To live, we must first die. Anybody who knows me understands that I often talk about death in my ministry but from the perspective of revival and resurrection. Paul talks about dying daily; in the same manner, death should be a daily process for us. We should rise to die to anything that is not like Christ. We should die to anything that keeps us being more like Him. When my husband and I counsel couples, we tell them their wedding day is also their first funeral. That day they commit to dying to themselves so that they can start the process of becoming one.

Those types of death are beneficial because both produce a greater reward due to the sacrifice to leave things behind necessary for your future. But yet, there's a place of death that I implore you not to be in during this season, and that is the "walking dead." Some exist but not living because they said "no" to God when they should've said "yes." As a result, what they are experiencing has caused them to exist but not truly live to their full potential. Discern well in this season what deserves your "yes" and "no." Because, when you leave here, you must be sure that you leave empty and not full on latent potential. Live well so you can leave well!

Live, Live, Live!!!

This illustration represents God dealing with the Jewish people through the prophet Ezekiel. These people were familiar with being in situations where they had not lived up to the standard God had set before them. They did not make the most of their heritage, but even in the midst of their bondage, God says to them, "Live!" Ezekiel 16 also stands as a parable revealing how God shares the story of an infant through Ezekiel, depicting that even in a helpless state, the graciousness of God is provided for those He loves. His nature is to reveal His love even when His people turn their back or fail to abide by His established standard. He remains gracious enough to show up and take care of His own.

In today's church, many of us are in the same condition.

We are worthy of comparison. We, like them, are in a state of emergency. God affirms our call to "Live" instead of upholding the death experience we seemingly are encountering. Identity is so powerful and necessary to the core of our existence. Therefore, when an identity crisis exists, we lack proper human function mainly because our identity speaks to our proper function. Again, if we are not fully aware of the identity of a thing, we will not understand its function. Your ability to function directly relates to your understanding of who you are. Lastly, the level of your functionality relies on understanding your identity.

Proper Identification Equals Proper Function And Produces Proper Outcomes

When we fail to identify with what we are called to do, we fail to function properly. We are devoid of energy, passion, vigor, and zeal in life and often aimlessly wander through life without purpose. The admonishment to "Live!" in Ezekiel 16:6 counteracts the lifelessness of those wallowing in their blood.

In many cases, what has caused us to bleed is what we are most likely to identify with versus what has caused us to live. Our blood connects us with our DNA, as it is the strongest indicator of identity. Through our bloodline passes, things are both good and bad. This is evidence of our generational blessings as well as generational curses. This evidence exists to reveal the deficiencies and the inheritances granted through our bloodline. Everything passed through our bloodline that doesn't serve to bless us will hinder us if left undetected and unresolved. If we leave these issues unresolved, they have the potential to prevent our forward momentum and the full potentiality of our becoming.

For many of us, the pain and the issues that have left us in our blood have been the main interruption to our identity. The pain of losing relationships, finances, status, dreams deferred, and sorrows in all forms have kept us lying in our blood and unable to move forward. However, the remedy is to live as God has called you to accept what he says about you. The blood is an illustration of who we are and a further reminder of what God did for us at Calvary. For without the shedding of blood, there is no remission of sins! His blood sanctifies and redeems us and cleanses us from all unrighteousness.

In that manner, "Living" beyond the identity crisis, the things that have come to distance you from your true sense of self and purpose, will require you no longer wallow in dead things. Grabbing hold of something that produces life causes you to rise out of crisis moments and commands you to "Live."

Acts 17:28 (NKJV)
"For in him we live and move and have our being."

1 Peter 2:9
"But you are a chosen generation, a royal priesthood, a holy nation, His own special people, that you may proclaim the praises of Him who called you out of darkness into His marvelous light;." (NKJV)

Ephesians 2:10
"For we are His workmanship, created in Christ Jesus for good works, which God prepared beforehand that we should walk in them."

Live Beyond Your Experience

The first priority of those who desire revival is to be familiar and acquainted with who they truly are beyond what they have experienced. The things that caused you to bleed cannot be the primary focus of your assignment, destination, or the purpose God has outlined for your life. Instead, employ prayer to assist you with speaking a different existence in your life. Prophecy beyond your past, and speak to your future! You have the ability to partner with Holy Spirit to move beyond the pain and experiences of the past.

Prayer:

Father, I have experienced crisis moments and states of emergency situations in my life that caused me to feel that I would not overcome, pull through, or be able to do what you were asking of me.

Honestly, even more than just doing your will, I often lacked the impetus to live the life you were calling me to. I repent, shift my focus away from the things that have attempted to hinder me in times past, move forward to becoming and doing what you require of me.

My decision today is to "live" and not just to live a mundane life, but one that qualifies me for the original intent and design of who you required me to be from the beginning. God send a revival within me that causes me to "LIVE!

CHAPTER FIVE

Illusion Breakers

Nothing teaches us about the preciousness of the Creator as much as when we learn the emptiness of everything else.

CHARLES HADDON-SPURGEON

When revival visits us, and God begins an inner work within, He pulls back all the layers and addresses the things that have us bound. One of the fallacies of our generation is the failure to deal with reality and truth. So much of what we present of ourselves is indeed based on pseudo-imagery, false narratives, prototypes of who we truly are, and misrepresentations of every kind. Social media is not the blame altogether…social media just provided us the platform to make false premises appear real.

Revivalists must be prepared to discern correctly between what is real and what is false. This process is more about discerning what's happening with others than dealing with what's happening in our lives. When emotional healing occurs for the revivalist, the ability to impact change in others increases tremendously.

Leave Wonderland

Many of us live in a fantasy world similar to Alice in Wonderland. We know that as a result of Alice living in Wonderland, she ends up landing in a world that is not hers. She becomes engaged in a culture, a world that is paradoxical to what she knew and understood the world to be.

People who have endured tremendous wounds are often easily captivated by living this existence. In many cases, their disassociation from reality started in their childhood as a means of escape from the real world or the reality of what was happening in their world. Tragically, our generation has produced so many that were mishandled in childhood and were subject to use escapism as their only means of survival.

Many believers deal with orphan spirits because their mother or father rejected them, and they've yet to identify with Christ as Father as part of their Christian heritage. The orphan spirit is so prevalent in our churches that it requires a book within itself to fully assist so many that have been subject to an identity crisis as a result of this level of rejection, abandonment, and absenteeism that accompanies it.

Despite failed parental relationships, many people are wounded because of failure in all types of relationships. However, a good look within will reveal that some of these same relationships were built on fantasy expectations that were impossible to maintain, particularly in our own relationships. When one party declines the offer to participate in the fantasy, the initiating party is hurt by the lack of participation.

Here's the crux of the matter, if the relationship was built on a fantasy, then the reality is you were not wounded by the person that failed to be a part of the relationship. The failure of the fantasy created the hurt, the wound. From that vantage point, our wounds should be viewed as internal, not external, as they originated within. We're not wounded by the non-playing individual as much as ourselves. This narrative serves as self-sabotage. That person just kept being who they truly were all along. But the distance between fantasy and reality was ultimately severed by the truth or reality of the non-existent relationship.

When Fitting In Doesn't Work

Because of the fantasy culture created in this generation, many people are caught looking for where they fit in and who their "group" is. I am a die-hard component of being a part of the right "company, tribe, association, network, etc." However, the tragedy of this search applies to those who are battle-torn by rejection, as they will often connect with the wrong people.
 by rejection, as they will often connect with the wrong people.

They desire a specific outcome that the rejected individual believes will heal their condition. The tragedy is they later find out that those individuals cannot fix what is broken within. As revivalists, sometimes fitting in is not the answer. God brings you to a certain situation, environment, or people with the requirement for you not to "fit in" but to be instead the change or the example necessary to promote change within that entity.

I have dealt with not fitting in personally. I know what it looks like to feel like what you have on the inside is valuable, but no one sees or understands. When I was among certain people, I could be in the room, in the circle, but not in the room and not in the circle. The thing that God healed for me is to understand how "fitting in" is not always what he desires. Sometimes, not fitting in or confirming to a space, group, or room allows you to add dimension to the room, whether acknowledged or not. From that point, I no longer desired conformity or acceptance as much as I desired to be one that can add to the room or space instead. What God may be calling you to do requires you to provoke change, and fitting in would require your assimilation versus the power of transformation.

Rejection and abandonment issues have to be healed from the inside out. If not, no group, church, family, association, or relationship will produce a deep sense of what belonging requires. This level of rejection will inhibit organic and authentic relationships and cause woundedness every time. We all must pass the rejection test and be mindful of "silent" offense.

Silent offense occurs when we are upset and perceive that we are being rejected. Once we embrace the suspicion that we are rejected, we are offended. Sometimes we will be offended and never confront the issue, acting like everything is okay when we engage with those we perceive rejected us, and that later becomes "silent offense." This is unhealthy, as the silent offense will deny confrontation of our issues and maximize the volume of rejection. Rejection is real, but it can protect us from relationships, doors, and situations that God did not intend for us to engage in. You can either allow rejection to serve you or break you. Sometimes what we think was designed to destroy us was intended to deliver, develop, and ultimately thrust us forward!

If relationships are built upon one individual's prescription to medicate their wounds, the relationship will fail tremendously unless both parties agree to the same medication. The moral of the story is the same. There is not one perfect group of people or perfect situation that will heal rejection. Furthermore, if you enter relationships expecting others to heal your rejection issues, hurt is once again inevitable. The realization that most people lack the capacity to heal us will bring us to the stark reality that most healing begins within and with the Father.

Issues stemming from rejection are not the only case of illusion. Fantasy and illusion are rampant in our culture, even within individuals with a healthy sense of self. Models of comparison, poor self-esteem, lack of confidence, and deferred dreams plague many of us daily. We are paralyzed, stagnant, and occasionally unable to move forward because we prefer fantasy over the real practical work required to make dreams come to pass. We want companionship but don't want to do the work to make them work. We desire entrepreneurship, but we don't desire the requirement of blood, sweat, and tears that goes along with it. We want a ministry, but we don't want the sacrifice, commitment, or challenge accompanying it.

Dismantle All Illusions

One of the things that the Lord began to deal with me during my continual process of becoming was the need to dismantle all illusions. There were things that I never wanted to do in ministry because of what I have observed over the years. These observations sometimes were mind-boggling. Then there were the seasons where I could not accept who God called me to be because I feared "success." Yep, you got it right; I said, "success."

Many of us are scared to do "well." We are afraid that if we succeed that we will not be able to maintain, sustain, or continue along the path of success. When we look closer at the relationship with the "fear of success," we find issues of independence, pride, and fear of rejection are also added to the equation. Maybe we believe God called us to something, but we don't fully trust him to bring it to pass, so we rely more on ourselves than on Him (independence). Maybe we fear success because we don't realize that there is an element of failure for every modicum of success.

We are afraid of the element of failure that could occur (pride). Then there is the thought process of what happens if I do "win?" What are they going to say? What are they going to do? We fear all the naysayers, the "they said's" that we know will stop pushing for us when we do become (fear of rejection). Several narratives and tapes we play internally cause us to live beneath or below God's standards for our lives. But we must be positioned to see what he sees.

On the other side of the coin is not only the illusions in our mind that are our constructs but also those that the enemy projects. His mission is to keep you from seeing the crystal-clear reality of who you truly are. He exists to get you off course, distracted, and distanced from your purpose. If he can get you to accept or take hold of his narrative, he will have accomplished exactly what he set out to do. Be reminded of 1 Peter 5:8; *"Be sober, be vigilant; because your adversary the devil, as a roaring lion, walketh about, seeking whom he may devour."* (KJV)

Let's take a look at two versions of 1 Corinthians 13:1-2:

For now, we see through a glass, darkly; but then face to face: now I know in part; but then shall I know even as also I am known. (KJV)

For now, we are looking in a mirror that gives only a dim (blurred) reflection [of reality as [a]in a riddle or enigma], but then [when perfection comes] we shall see in reality and face to face! Now I know in part (imperfectly), but then I shall know and understand [b]fully and clearly, even in the same manner as I have been [c]fully and clearly known and understood [[d]by God]. (AMP, Classic Edition)

The Looking Glass

The Apostle Paul speaks to the Corinthian church about seeing through a glass darkly. What does he wish to convey here? He is referring to a glass that is actually a mirror. However, during Paul's time, their mirrors were polished metal, and, in some instances, they were made of brass that required constant polishing. This glass had to be polished so often that they would attach a pumice stone to it to be available to polish when the time came.

Paul wrote this letter to the Corinthians because he knew they would understand the language. It was relevant to them since they were known for making this type of glass or mirror. The way I was able to relate to the illustration was to consider the "good silverware." You know, "the silverware" that your mama, grandma, or great aunt would pull out for special occasions that had been shined up after the last use and put up for the following memorable holiday.

This is the level of glass that Paul was referring to, which in our day would be similar to the type of mirror you would see at the fair in the House of Mirrors. It's like a puzzle or a riddle, an enigma translated into Greek. This glass is so distorted that what you see should be real, but its reflection is highly distorted. Your perception of the object distorts your ability to connect with the object's reality. So, what should be real is not seen, and what is false is what is seen.

There Appears To Be A Great Contradiction

Have you ever been in a season where the whole world appears to be a false representation of the reality you know should exist? Everything you have hoped for, waited for and believed God for is seemingly in direct opposition to what you are dealing with daily. A great contradiction between what is distorted and what's false appears more real. The enemy loves further to perpetuate this falsehood during our lives when everything we have established our faith upon is seemingly failing. So we end up with the great contradiction of life that troubles us as we go along.

Similarly, as Paul, we see evil is always before us, even when we want to do right. Even if we get on the right path, something is always there to distract or deter us. Even when we aren't deterred and walking the straight and narrow, the enemy is trying to afflict our bodies, touch our families, and disable our minds. We want to make sense of it all. We want to understand it all. We want God to tell us, "Why?"

We're like the little kid that asks his parents all day but why? Why God? Why is this happening? Why can't I see my way out? Why can't I see my way through? Why can't I see myself over? Why can't I see the finish line? Ecclesiastes 8:16-17 (MSG) says this, according to Solomon: "When I determined to load up on wisdom and examine everything taking place on earth, I realized that if you keep your eyes open day and night without even blinking, you'll still never figure out the meaning of what God is doing on this earth. Search as hard as you like; you won't make sense of it. No matter how smart you are, you won't get to the bottom of it".

The problem is, in many cases, this is not new advice; we are not seeing things through God's eyes. We will never see some things as He does until we begin to adapt to his way of doing, living, and being from a kingdom perspective. We must adopt a few behaviors to become revivalists who are also illusion breakers. First, we must combat faulty vision.

See Through Proper Lens

When our natural eyes create a blurred image of whatever we are looking at, it is called astigmatism. The word didn't exist in Paul's time, but he is describing this when trying to understand or make sense of life's circumstances. We suffer from mental astigmatism—our mental vision of what happens in our lives is often blurred. Our capacity for revelation is limited, and our accessibility to the revelation of our situation is also limited. If we avoid dealing with unresolved trauma, we will see life through a faulty lens, limiting our ability to be transformed.

Whenever you want more of a thing, you have to make more room for it, which is capacity. If you are praying and believing for God to do something different in your life, then you will have to make more room, storage, and capacity for Him. So how do you do this? We do this by walking out the word and doing the word of God.

James 1:23-25 tells us:

"For if anyone is a hearer of the word and not a doer, he is like a man observing his natural face in a mirror; for he observes himself, goes away, and immediately forgets what kind of man he was. But he who looks into the perfect law of liberty and continues in it, and is not a forgetful hearer but a doer of the work, this one will be blessed in what he does". (NKJV)

When I peer into the word of God and begin to do what the word of God says, I have more access to the power of God and the knowledge of who He is. While I already have come to grips with the reality that "His ways are not our ways, and His thoughts are not our thoughts, for they are higher than ours," then I can compensate for the fact that it's not my requirement to figure Him out but to respond to his instructions. The great thing about it is that He does not leave us hopeless or helpless. He has given us his word to demolish the partition between our limited sight, insight, and revelation and to bring us closer to seeing him "face to face," as the scriptures share in 1 Corinthians 13:12.

Overcome Fear & Rejection

As mentioned earlier, one of the primary things that hinder our vision and our ability to see things how God does is fear and rejection. Fear isolates us from the truth and causes us to believe that we are traveling through this paradoxical world by looking through the glass and never being a part of what is happening on the other side of the glass. Our situations perpetuate this futile cycle, and we experience life by always gazing and peering into what things may be instead of owning up to what they are.

Hebrews 11:1, "Now faith is the substance of things hoped for, the evidence of things not seen.." (NKJV)

If I employ faith in my circumstances, then I can automatically override fear and rejection with my faith. Now I can focus more on not being excluded, but on being included. He calls me "family." He grants us access to Him so that no matter what is going on in our journey, He is a part of it. He is here with us. We are not isolated. We are not rejected. We belong to Him. Then when I am overwhelmed by the contradictions, I must remember Isaiah 41:10 and 1 Peter 2:9:

Isaiah 41:10
Fear not, for I am with you; Be not dismayed, for I am your God. I will strengthen you, Yes, I will help you, I will uphold you with My righteous. (NKJV)

1 Peter 2:9
But you are a chosen generation, a royal priesthood, a holy nation, His own special people, that you may proclaim the praises of Him who called you. (NJKV)

Freed From Wonderland

Lastly, we must understand that by the nature of who we are and who we are, and by who He is, He requires us to operate as one with dual citizenship.

We're not called to make sense of this world but rather to stay in "training for reigning." He's preparing us for reigning now and with Him for eternity. This process of refining and purifying that we're going through is so that we can be the bride He is looking for. Pretty much, he is getting us all dolled up for his return.

God has considered all of our "ugly" places and peered behind the scenes at all our pain, hurt, worries, and fears, and yet He says, "Don't worry." I'm taking you through this thing called "life," you are not alone. While you are here, I am not wasting time with you but preparing you for the championship. I have you in boot camp because I am getting my best ready for my return.

am working on you while you are on Earth because I need you to have dominion here. As we are being prepared for His return, we will spend the rest of our days ruling and reigning. But also, while we are here, we get to enjoy what He did on the cross for us. The Bible says in Ephesians 2 that we used to be strangers, we didn't fully understand the covenants and what God has done for us, but He went to the cross and tore down the wall of partition that separated His people. We now have the same access to God because we are His family. In those times, I remember 2 Corinthians 4:17-18 (KJV):

> *"For our light affliction, which is but for a moment, worketh for us a far more exceeding and eternal weight of glory; while we look not at the things which are seen, but at the things*

which are not seen: for the things which are seen are temporal; but the things which are not seen are eternal."

Declarations:

My spiritual sight is being renewed, and I am dedicating myself back to God and to His word so that I can see clearly again.

I'm not living my life as one looking into the glass, but as I understand more about who God is, I know more about who I am. My capacity for all things has increased, and I am ready to come...(fill in your confession here).

I am overcoming my fear and rejection because it is an enemy of my faith, and if my faith is shaky, then I will open the door to isolation and loneliness.

I will not approach my life as one that does not have help or a savior. I am loved, I am enough, I am free, I am destined, I am purposed, and I AM REVIVAL!

God is recalibrating, re-shaping, re-focusing me, and making me ready to be an agent of change on the earth.

CHAPTER SIX

The Wilderness Experience

Study the History of Revival. God has Always Sent Revival in the Darkest Days. Oh, For A Mighty, Sweeping Revival Today!

ADRIAN ROGERS

Revival within causes you to believe in the power of destination over origin. No matter where you can from, God can use you to fulfill a specific assignment. Your genesis story is not strong enough to deny God's anointing, assignment, or call on your life. When you desire revival (inward change), you're more apt to realize everything you endure can be used to serve the greater purpose of your life.

Origins Don't Override Destination

Moses starts his life off in a place that could easily be associated with rejection instead of redemption. He was born when Pharaoh required all male children to be drowned in the Nile River, but Moses' life was spared because of the destiny appointment that Moses would later have with God. What was meant to destroy him was used to save him. He was rescued by Pharaoh's daughter and raised in the Egyptian courts under the same lineage that intended to take his life and was now sparing his life.

How do you view your story when you consider your beginnings and childhood? There may be less joyful situations, while others are fond memories of days gone by. True, many of us have endured horrific situations. However, it's all in how you look at the story. Do you see your life story as the glass is half empty or half full?

There are tragic situations that have happened to the people of God in and out of the church. Some of our stories are enough to declare that the fact that we are still alive is nothing short of a miracle. If you dwell on where you came from more than where you are going, you will always be stuck by your origination, your beginnings. We see this in the life of Moses. Ultimately his obedience to the assignment revealed that he didn't allow his origination to depreciate his destination.

Some Things Must Die

While appropriating change within, revival will also cause you to deal with the death of some things. After death, burial and resurrection are available. If we can deal with the end of things in our lives, then we appreciate the new things. Isaiah 43:19 states, "Behold, I will do a new thing; now it shall spring forth; shall ye not know it? I will even make a way in the wilderness and rivers in the desert."

Beyond Moses' childhood, he finds himself in a situation that causes his life to take yet another turn. Moses' observation of an Egyptian beating a man of Hebrew descent caused Moses to become a murderer. When Moses killed the Egyptian that day, he went all in. He didn't employ strategy, no plan of action, nor did he consult anyone. When you have not mastered impulse control or the things that drive your innate nature, you will struggle in ministry, in being a change agent, and in everyday life.

That is why God allows us to be placed in situations that require the things within us to be fleshed out at the root. Maturity requires we learn how to properly respond to the things that offend, anger, frustrate, and upset us. Some of the things we are confronted with simply doesn 't require a response. Our best response may be silence, prayer, or finding a better time to address the issue.

The Wilderness Will Force You Into Your Destiny

After hiding the man in the sand, Moses fled to the backside of the desert. The desert is rendered in Hebrew as "midbar" or "wilderness." According to Exodus 3:1, the desert's backside is the "region behind a man," and the east is the region in front. Moses essentially found himself in a place signified by what was "behind the man" his past, indiscretions, failures, flaws, etc. We find ourselves in wilderness situations looking to escape what is behind us. That is where God often meets us and graces us for what's next. God uses our wilderness wanderings as the place where He propels us into destiny.

After hiding the man in the sand, Moses fled to the backside of the With preparation; we will be ready for promotion. We often fail to obtain promotions because we need to understand preparation. Instead of getting the value out of the wilderness, we talk ourselves into being stuck there. This devastates our arrival. In that regard, when promotion time comes, we have failed to address what God desired to "flesh out" of us. When you find yourself in the wilderness, rejoice...know that this is most likely where God came to destroy the "unnecessary" privately before He elevates you openly.

Death Is Inevitable

God does not take us to the desert to ultimately destroy us, but so we can die to ourselves. The wilderness is a place of solace, refuge, cutting, and refinement. In our dying process, we posture ourselves for resurrection and transformation. However, when God gets ready to prepare us in a particular area that correlates with our purpose and destiny, He often takes us to a barren place because on the other side of death is life. Death may be inevitable in several areas for this next place you are assigned to.

Intentional focus is required to accommodate your next move and will ensure you're not stuck bringing your past into your future. One of the main hindrances to our future success is that we attempt to hold on to the same tools, resources, and relationships that were proven unfruitful in our past, yet we hang on. Let dead things die. There are things that God has ordered for your life that must die! On the flip side there are also things we've allowed to die within us that must live. A wise person understands and knows the difference.

Without this process, many of us would allow an ill-informed mindset to dictate our destiny. What does it mean to have an ill-informed mindset? This is where we have not properly dealt with "us" We have not addressed the "issues" that hold us back. For most of us, when we have this conversation with others and inquire about what is holding them back, they will most likely start talking about everything that has happened from the perspective of what everyone has done to them.

A place of death requires that you see your life not through the lens of what everyone else has done to you but what you allowed. What role did you play? Yes, some things have happened to all of us that were outside of our control. However, there is still a place in your response that removes the control or power of what they did (past) to what you will do (future). You can't control what everyone around you is doing or has done. But you can control the person that you confront daily... yourself. Forward momentum always requires a crossroads moment. This is where you decide what must live and what must die in order for you to "crossover" into your destined place."

When God Doesn't Make Sense

Moses was at a crossroads moment. The necessity of his obedience would change his life forever. It was at this moment that God placed Moses on assignment. The times that we most likely expect not to be used by God are often the times when He calls for us. The irony of God's decision-making process regarding us appears as though He is impractical at times. We are being processed by a God who declares, *"For my thoughts are not your thoughts, neither are your ways my ways."*

> *Isaiah 55:8 "For my thoughts are not your thoughts, neither are your ways my ways" (NIV)*

Ultimately, we shouldn't try to figure Him out; our human intelligence is no match for His divinity.

When God calls us, He places us on a mission. We have to deal with the harsh reality of death (dying to ourselves) and the harsh reality of not understanding his plan. He is the God that asks you to sign up for something that he did not confirm all the details of. In our times, we know that wisdom requires us to "read before you sign." It's our duty to read the small print, the big print, and all the print in between.

Wisdom prompts the desire for understanding and knowledge of any assignment. We want to know what we are signing up for and what happens if what we signed up should fail. God doesn't play into our requirements on most occasions. He will assign a task without fully outlining all the details. Most of us are keenly acquainted with this process and understand it thoroughly. We must realize that this is where we must have faith and trust in the vision, mandate, and mission that He sets before us—the miraculous hinges upon your obedience. When you obey, God will perform.

God Is Not Concerned With Our Conveniences

Moses' story is interesting because God chooses to use him in the later days of his life when his focus is on comfort and settling down. It appears that God enjoys interrupting our comfort. Moses most likely thinks his life should be defined by a "rocking chair"; however, God is thinking "deliverer." After his burning bush experience, Moses is dedicated to making practical sense out of the impractical.

When God called you, He didn't do it on the premise of what was convenient for you but instead on what he already predestined for you. He considered you before you ever got in trouble, before you messed up before you stole the car, before you had the abortion, before you fornicated, and before you took that drink. He appointed you before you entered college and before you dropped out. You were already on His mind.

Moses envisioned himself as the guy who tended the sheep. That was his gig. He was an outsider, didn't fit in with the Hebrews or the Egyptians, and didn't fit in with the Midianites. On top of that, he was slow in speech; Moses stuttered. I can imagine Moses thinking, "Lord, why did you choose me to be the one to bring the people out? I can further envision him saying, "Really, God, who does that? His question was not unreasonable. Many of us have done the same thing because we don't feel qualified. We have counted ourselves out in times past because we did not feel we were good enough, and it prevented us from rising to the occasion or challenge set before us.

In his humanity, Moses looks for the practicality in the situation and starts a dialogue with God. Like us, he wants to be affirmed. He does not want to go to the arena, get on the stage, propose a solution, and then get the tomatoes hurled at him. Nobody wants to do that. We prefer that folks are willing to listen to what we say when we get to the stage. Moses asks, "God, what have you established for that?" What do you have in mind? Are you going to talk to them in their sleep? Do they know what I'm supposed to look like when I come? Who's emceeing and presiding at this event? Will there be security there if Pharaoh gets upset and wants to smite me? What am I supposed to wear? As a matter of fact, who shall I tell them sent me?

God tells Moses to tell them that the one who sent him is the "I am who I am." This is what you are to say to the Israelites: 'I am has sent me to you." At that moment, God is less concerned with who Moses deems himself to be, but instead who God is "in" Moses. He demonstrates to Moses that he is the God that equips those He calls. The name that the "called of God" go in is not their own, but His. God promises Moses something better than self-confidence. He promises him God-confidence instead. He promises Moses His presence, namesake, and authority will be with him.

When God starts to work revival in you, He will remind you of who you are and who you are in Him. This identification process sets us free and establishes what is required to fulfill the purpose. When you experience God speaking about your future, you can never go back to who you were in times past. Of course, you may not have a literal "burning bush," but you can expect a life-changing experience the moment you say "yes to His will."

What's In Your Hand?

According to Exodus 4, God finally let Moses in on a secret. While he is trying to understand whether or not the people will receive him, God asks him what's in your hand? The problem here is that what Moses had in his hand was dead. It was an inanimate object, void of life. But when he threw the staff on the ground as directed by God, it became a snake. God shows Moses that no matter what the situation, everything that he needs is already provided.

At this point, all of his arguments are dismantled. All of His desires to dodge the call mean nothing. When God is ready to use you, once you have endured the process of death and your wilderness experience, He activates His glory and power in you. From there, you will demonstrate God's miraculous power to those who don't believe. What's in your hand? What do you possess that God can use to perform the exceptional, amazing, extraordinary, unique, unusual, and incredible, unconventional through you?

Sign On The Dotted Line......

The fact of the matter is that ministry is just like that. The fact you can still muster up the strength to get out of bed every morning after all you have seen and after all you have been through is nothing short of amazing. Furthermore, the fact that you gave God a "yes," after all the hell you had to pay, is nothing short of the greatest miracle in your life. Who signs up for the gauntlet? Who signs up for a mission that will keep you up at night? Cause you to lose friends and most likely be isolated from those you love? Who signs up for what will ultimately be the death of you before you experience the resurrection of the same thing? Who signs up for something that will cost you everything, and you don't know what the price tag looks like? Who signs up for something that will cause your family to walk away for seasons of uncertainty, rejection, loss, and pain? Who signs up for that?

You Are Equipped!

However, some believe they are called to be Glory Carriers, Change Agents, Trailblazers, and Revialists on the earth. These people are supernaturally equipped and empowered by God and His work in the last days. This is the generation that God is pouring out His spirit on all flesh. God is looking for a great army of people willing to take up the mandate of impacting change. He is raising revivalists who think outside the box and look for new ways of hosting God's glory on earth. Such are we!

Prayer:

Father, I accept your mission, mandate, and assignment for my life. I will be the first to admit I have struggled with what you require me to do.

At times it's overwhelming and frustrating, and I lack the comprehension of how this fits my life's big picture. But today, I am willing to put all my issues aside to obey your will.

I have counted the costs and realized my obedience is better than sacrifice. Everything I have been through has been difficult, but I now see how the wilderness and the burning bush experiences have shaped and refined who I am today.

Thank you for considering me as one you desire to use to carry your glory on the earth!

CHAPTER SEVEN

Scar Revealers

How we have prayed for a revival-We did not care whether it was old-fashioned or not. What we asked for was that it should be such that would cleanse and revive His children and set them on fire to win others.

MARY BOOTH

Once you dealt with the wounds, there is the question of the scars. In the body of Christ, the narrative for the wounded, the church hurt, the guilted, and those who are ashamed can be predominant in many conversations. The key to healing in most of those narratives is transparency. As a revivalist, once you have endured the process of healing and wholeness, God will have you reach back to others to be a testament to your victory.

However, herein lies the tragedy; It is hard for the saints of God to endure the storm and then to testify of the storm from a raw and gritty place. We are more apt to talk about what everybody else did during the storm and less likely to discuss our role. Yes, some of us have endured tremendous injustice, mistreatment, abuse, and deep places of hurt and pain. But rather than being open and honest about the pain, we have learned how to cover our scars so that no one will see the mark and evidence of what we have been through.

It would be beneficial, to be honest enough to show others our scars openly. After all, they are a sign that the wound has healed but a reminder that the hurt truly occurred. John 20:19-31 (KJV) reveals to us a few thought processes regarding how we benefit from our scars. The Bible reveals in the passage of scriptures below this narrative of John 20:19-31 (NKJV)

> *19 Then the same day at evening, being the first day of the week, when the doors were shut where the disciples were assembled for fear of the Jews, came Jesus and stood in the midst, and saith unto them, Peace be unto you. 20 And when he had so said, he shewed unto them his hands and his side. Then were the disciples glad, when they saw the Lord. 21 Then said Jesus to them again, Peace be unto you: as my Father hath sent me, even so send I you. 22 And when he had said this, he breathed on them, and saith unto them, Receive ye the Holy Ghost: 23 Whose soever sins ye remit, they are remitted unto them; and whose soever sins ye retain, they are retained. 24 But Thomas, one of the twelve, called Didymus, was not with them when Jesus came. 25 The other disciples therefore said unto him, We have seen the Lord. But he said unto them, Except I shall see in his hands the print of the nails, and put my finger into the print of the nails, and thrust my hand into his side, I will not believe. 26 And after eight days again his disciples were within, and Thomas with them: then came Jesus, the doors being shut, and stood in the midst, and said, Peace be unto you. 27 Then saith he to Thomas, Reach hither thy finger, and behold my hands; and reach hither thy hand, and thrust it into my side: and be not faithless, but believing. 28 And Thomas answered and said unto him, My Lord and my God. 29 Jesus saith unto him, Thomas, because thou hast*

seen me, thou hast believed: blessed are they that have not seen, and yet have believed. 30 And many other signs truly did Jesus in the presence of his disciples, which are not written in this book: 31 But these are written, that ye might believe that Jesus is the Christ, the Son of God; and that believing ye might have life through his name.

One of the first considerations was Jesus accommodation for peace in the text. In the narrative, Jesus recites "Peace be with you" three times. Because of the nature of this language, we think nothing about it. However, there is more to the meaning of the phrase, "peace be with you."

The "Peace be with you" statement from Jesus held a greater depth of meaning, which was common in His day. It went beyond the general "Hey," "What's up," and "Howdy," but meant, may you have peace, complete healing, and wholeness. It is as though there was a requirement for greetings to have a greater meaning than the way our generation ascribes meaning to our daily salutations. It is apparent there was a greater concern in Jesus' day to greet each other with more than a simple acknowledgment of presence but a declaration of wellness and wholeness.

"Peace be with you" actually means "Shalom." According to Strong's Concordance, "7965," shalom means completeness, wholeness, health, peace, welfare, safety, soundness, tranquility, prosperity, perfectness, fullness, rest, harmony, and the absence of agitation or discord. Shalom comes from the root verb shalom, meaning to be complete, perfect, and full.

When you desire the peace that only God can give you, that is shalom. God is the one that only grants peace but makes us whole. We can speak peace into our lives and the lives of others. When we gather together as a church, we're unaware or cognizant of others' need for healing and wholeness. We're dealing with our stuff, rushing in to do "church," and failing to realize the benefit of being "church." This allows us to easily overlook each other, and we need to offer simple words of encouragement and admonishment that will push our brother or sister in Christ to make it through the week. These words can be just what is needed to push our brother and sister in Christ to make it through the upcoming week. However, sometimes we may find that we are more apt to pour salt on wounds instead of offering the simple words of healing such as "peace be unto you."

Because of the lack of transparency and confidence in our church communities, we are less likely to share our trials, difficulties, and even deliverance testimonies. We fear being judged, criticized, or tragic because our testimony is shared without consent. However, we should seek to find mature believers to partner in our healing process. The Bible admonished us in James 5:16, "Therefore confess our faults to others and then commit to pray as well.

I will never forget when a lady I know came to confess some of the things she was going through and how they were the source of arrested development. As she shared, not only was I able to listen and speak life to hear, but I began to feel this sense of freedom about some issues in my life. Her testimony was intended to set her free and release her bondage, but it set me free.

I admired her strength and desire to share her struggle as a way of removing the weight of secrecy. Secrecy has a way of keeping us in place of arrested development. Secrecy ultimately hinders us from being free. Without freedom, our ability as a revivalist to serve as the weight of guilt and shame tremendously impacts change agents. We don't get a trophy for going through our lives without wounds, but we get the reward of freedom for dealing with our wounded places.

Something Has Attempted To Break Us

When we consider our wounds, we realize that what happened to us in some way also scarred us. In some cases, this has resulted in arrested development. We've yet to mature or develop to where we should be because we are stuck or paralyzed by our past. However, a paradigm shift will help us to see how often what was intended to destroy us was used to make us.

In the resurrection narrative, Jesus shows up after the resurrection and allows the disciples to see the His scars. This narrative is of great interest to me. If we can explore the reality that most of us have experienced some situation that felt like the death and burial of us, then we most likely have desired a resurrection moment. That is when we expect some retribution or vindication for what's been done to us. We expect to see a better day going forward than the days we have experienced in times past. We desire a third-day experience that will supersede all of the pain, hurt, trauma, and negative dealings of the past.

The difference between Jesus and us is that we are not as interested in showing up amongst our family and friends with proof of what seemingly was our "crucifixion" moment. But yet, Jesus appears before the disciples with testimony and recognition of who He was and the evidence of what had been done to him through his scars. Thomas was not there on that first occasion, but he failed to believe when the others told him. A week later, Jesus shows up, and while Thomas still does not believe, Jesus allows him to see his scars. Jesus is not ashamed of the things that attempted to break Him. He proves that He has power over death, hell, and the grave. Of course, Jesus is the only one who endured this pain as the Savior to a dying world. It benefits all to see the willingness of Jesus to show his scars.

The first question one ponders is why Jesus showed his

wounds and scars. Then there is a deeper question requiring examination; why did Jesus have wounds? It seems more logical that the Christ that had conquered death and the grave would not appear injured but whole. I would expect He would look resurrected, which in my mind's eye means He would appear perfected, refined, and new. Essentially this resurrected Jesus would be perfect! After all, he just defeated death with the ultimate victory. Could it be that Jesus understood the importance of showing His scars not only as a confirmation of His identity but as validation of his victory? Secondly, while they had been in mourning for him while struggling with grief and loss, was the showing of his scars a sign they were wounded together?

Jesus had survived at the cross, the taunting, the lies, the criticism, and the failure of the people around Him to acknowledge who He truly was. The disciples had lost a friend, a brother, and a savior, and their pains were immense as well. When we show others our scars, we allow them not only to understand what we came through but instead of what we overcame! What didn't kill us worked only to make us stronger.

When we have scars, there is proof that a wound has occurred. If you have a serious wound, a scar remains as proof of the wound. There are some scars that are so deep on our physical body that others can identify us simply by our scars. Some people are known by a scar on their face, the scar on their leg, on their hand, etc. When asked about the scar, they have a story to tell. The story represents details of the origination of the scar, how old the scar is, the process that occurred for healing the scar, and so on. However, not only do physical scars define us, but emotional ones do as well. These are a bit tricky because it is the scars on the inside that we fight the hardest to hide. We protect those scars because they point to a certain incident, occurrence, or trauma. In most cases, we are not as willing as Jesus to reveal our scars.

In regards to emotional hurts, many of us still have wounds because we have not allowed the salve of forgiveness to heal the wound, so no scar has formed. The scar is a sign that there was once a scab. That scab was there to protect the wound for a certain period of time, and once it has fallen off, all that remains is the calloused area. This calloused area is no longer as fragile as the skin that was originally there.

Once the scab is gone and healing occurs, the likelihood of that calloused skin being damaged as severely as before lessens. That place has already taken a hit, and while it is still subject to pain, it is not as easily injured as before. The problem with emotional wounds is that we don't realize how often the emotional wounds that we fight to hide are more visible than others. We would like to believe this is not the case. However, often we are in denial that the injury still exists.

Then there are spiritual wounds, we may have been hurt in church, or we may have prayers that seem to be unanswered. We may feel trapped in a cycle of sin that further leads to guilt and condemnation. As a result, we've lost faith or the ability to receive or understand God's grace. We need help to connect with others in ministry, or we become territorial. Sometimes we are territorial because we prioritize the church's culture as the primary context we relate to. As a result, we use our wounds as a mechanism to rebel, control, manipulate, and deny the existence of our pain.

Some have been hurt in the church and their very own homes. Some have encountered deep sexual and physical abuse, so these wounds are not easy to overcome. They take longer to heal and a deeper process of restoration to overcome. Jesus, however, shows them his scars because His scars remind them that He has overcome death regardless of what He went through. The good news is: Jesus did not have to heal Himself.

God raised Him from the dead and allowed the scars to stay as proof of what He endured and overcame. God did not perform any surgery; He allowed Jesus' scars and wounds to remain.

1) To deal with our woundedness. We must first acknowledge that we have been injured. We must name what has hurt us and deal with the root of the issue without denial. When we have a physical wound, we may feel pain, but we don't want to look at it in most cases. But with our emotional wounds and scars, we must look intently at them and see them for what they truly are. We must address what is at the root and the core of our hurt…what happened? What really happened?

2) Secondly, we need a relationship with our Heavenly Father, whereby we rely on Him as the source of inner healing. There are times in this phase when nobody can "fix" us. The healing we require is found in God alone. The master surgeon is Jesus Christ. While he is working on us, we must do our best to keep the wound clean, dry, and free from being infected again.

3) Our wounds are kept free and healing takes place by the obvious for every believer…forgiveness. Walking in forgiveness and love is the best assurance we have against wounds being opened again.

However, healing does not take place in a vacuum. God has given each of us the power to be wounded healers. We may be wounded, but God can still use us to assist someone else in their healing process. Thomas doubts that the man before him is Jesus, so he wants to see the scars. Revivalists will encounter people unwilling to believe that the God you serve can also heal, particularly if they cannot witness our scars. Essentially, your testimony, your life story, and what you have been through are the best witness of the power of God and His operation in your life. This generation needs to see real, transparent, authentic people who are unafraid to show their scars. Revivalists are not ashamed to say they are not what they used to be but by the grace of God. Some people are waiting for you to show them how you conquered your "valley of the shadow of death" moment and came out on the other side. Show them your scars!

Freedom is found in knowing that you are not scarred alone. No one wants to come off the battlefield and feel like they are the only ones injured. We prefer a mantra that states, "You show me your scars, and I will show you mine." We place less value on people who have seemingly never been through anything. In our humanity, it is hard to believe someone can help us if they have not endured anything. That is why transparency is so paramount. Let's stop hiding and be more willing to come out from our wounded places and express what it looks like to be the one who overcame.

It is often that the glory of the Lord is revealed in broken places. God shows himself mighty not to the independent and perfected but to the broken and those who acknowledge their need for Him.

Psalms 51:17 says, "The sacrifices of God are a broken spirit, A broken and a contrite heart— These, O God, You will not despise". (NKJV)

Upon our return to transparency and removal of our facades, we can facilitate a place of recalibration and renewal for the lost. This transparency has to go beyond our mid-week service testimony. In our discipleship model, we should be "free" to "free" others—free people, "free" people. When we can move past the fear of our checkered past, we know we are genuinely delivered and not returning to those places. As a result, the power resides within that will help us to guide others along a path of restoration. We have often been unable to share at this level because we are still bound. We must move past the wounds so what remains will only be our scars.

Your wounds are those places that are not yet healed. They are still a work in progress, so we have guarded them so much. Your scars, however, represent the place of victory and triumph. You may still be working on some of your wounds, but time is too short for those who need you to wait until everything in your life is perfect. Let others see that you are still a work in progress instead of attempting to appear whole. God uses broken people to help other broken people.

Questions:

1. Are there areas in my life that I should acknowledge as wounds? What is the root cause of those wounds?

_____

_____

_____

_____

_____

_____

_____

2. Have I dealt with those areas in prayer and confession?

3. Who do I need to forgive, release, potentially restore, or move away from?

4. What (soul) work do I still need to do to ensure I feel free enough to share my story?

CHAPTER EIGHT

Flight Training

> *Revival is a renewed conviction of sin and repentance, followed by an intense desire to live in obedience to God. It is giving up one's will to God in deep humility.*
>
> CHARLES FINNEY

Revivalists are called to soar! Soaring requires a success metric that assumes the posture of overcoming difficulties to rise above negative circumstances. Becoming one that soars is only sometimes the easiest thing to do, as it requires identifying the things that keep you grounded.

However, the benefit of revival is inward change. We must also be aware that while revival can supernaturally promote heart change, there are occasions when what has hindered us from moving forward may require not only the work of self-deliverance but also soul care. Sometimes when we've been grounded for so long professional help is necessary to give us the wings needed to fly again. Success is the language of the revivalist, and God elevates the revivalist to a place of success and favor when they live their everyday life as a matter of revival or change.

Obedience Is The Language Of The Kingdom

First, let's step back and define God's metric and standard for success. It can get tricky in the Body of Christ since many of us have acquainted success with our standards. Things that indicate success to us culturally are not necessarily relevant in the Kingdom of God. God is not as concerned with our numbers, likes, statuses, programming, theology, or popularity. Our obedience and submission to fulfilling kingdom mandates are meaningful to Him. Whatever He is saying and requires of you is what he will ultimately deem a success for you.

Relinquish Comparisons

Much of what we consider greatness is determined by how we value one's material success. However, many of us still need to catch up by chasing what we thought was an indicator or higher mark of success based on others' achievements. Don't misjudge your value or those around you in this season because you don't "look" like or they don't "look" like what you deem the model of "made it" to be. There is a high price to seek affirmation from those who can't comprehend who you are because you seemingly have not accomplished what they deem successful at this juncture.

Take Flight

We are in a season where God is calling us to "take flight" and to encounter Him so that we soar and rise to the place he has assigned us to live in. This time when you take flight, you will not soar on occasion, but God will elevate you to a higher place in him where he will require you to live. This change of location and destination starts within as we become more accustomed to not living in a place of dysfunction, indecision, double-mindedness, woundedness, pain, disbelief, unforgiveness, and the like. However, this is the place that He will require us to live in to accomplish the revival mandate upon our lives.

Webster defines soaring as "increasing rapidly above the usual level." What we must realize is that soaring is a place that requires a level of momentum, meaning that once you start to soar, you must stay on a steady level to increase rapidly above the usual level. Occasionally, a problem exists for those who have been processed by God to soar above the ordinary, to be a part of the uncommon and the unusual. The problem appears once we receive a mandate or sense the inward witness of God calling us to something greater. We tend to desire flight immediately. However, to soar, you have to climb first. Nobody starts off soaring. There is a process that promotes you to the soaring level. You must walk before you crawl. If you are in this for the long haul, you must jog before you run. Soaring is a progressive movement that takes time if you want to continue on a path of soaring.

The question you must consider is; who wants to soar and then be forced to come down from the soaring place? This movement now requires accelerating not rapidly above the usual level but slowly behind the normal level, consistent with elevation. To soar is to be unusual, uncommon, and extraordinary. It is to do what everyone can't do. When you progress to the place of inward change and preparation for revival within, you will be required to soar and take flight! The Bible says of soaring, in Isaiah 40:31 in the NIV Version;

> *"But those who wait on the Lord Shall renew their strength; They shall mount up with wings like eagles, They shall run and not be weary, They shall walk and not faint."(NKJV).*

Revivalists are leaders; they are transformers and change agents. If you allow your life to minister to others, there are some things you will have to soar above. That means you will have to hold onto your call as you wait for God to manifest all He said He would do in your life.

The Process Proceeds Success

Sometimes we're so busy trying to get to the stage and the pulpit or to be affirmed and acknowledged that we fail to focus on the important things to be free and not be weighted down. We desire success but deny the process. Who says our success in God is contingent upon doing any of these things in ministry? What if the journey is just as valuable or even more so than the destination? Because the journey, the waiting, and the hoping allowed you to understand how to walk and not faint, how not to be weary in well doing, to believe to see the goodness of the Lord in the land of the living! As a result, you will soar like an eagle when your day comes. But we are so busy getting there that the process God has defined became a burden when He intended it to be a blessing for our soaring place.

To rush to our destination, we can become impatient and push God to release us into our assignment without a complete process. We are impatient because we feel ineffective if we're not actively working on our gifts or not doing what we think we should. However, mastery requires that you hone your gifts. Successful people always work their gifts with or without platforms or audiences. They read, observe, train, and prepare themselves behind the scenes. When the door of opportunity opens, they are not caught off guard but ready to walk right through the open door.

They Didn't Clip Your Wings. Own Your Soar.

It's hard to be who you are called to be when you believe the honing of your gift is the responsibility of others. If your excuse is they didn't show me, teach me, or tell me this or that; then you have not invested enough time in the background learning your craft. When you are called to it, you will be ready for it when invited to the table. Mentorship is powerful, but it is only as good as application. Often, people are deceived into believing they need something more when they have not invested in themselves on their own. A mentor became a mentor because they endured a process of apprenticeship, accountability, action, and application of what they have learned.

With closer examination, you'll realize that your gifts were not buried. They were just being planted. God is an intentional God who is not in the habit of being wasteful. He will return for whatever he put in you at the right time. We are so busy trying to show the world our gifts that we have not allowed God to bloom what he planted.

Sometimes when we're in the infancy stages of our gifts, we rush to share them with the world. Our society orders overexposure as the construct of the day. Everybody wants to be seen doing something. We rush to show the world what we think is a plant when God says, "Wait, right now, you only have a bud." I know there are some things that you have been plowing at for years, and you and I would hate to think that God only calls it a "bud." How tragic, right? But God is a God of wisdom, and when he plants you, it may feel like you are being buried, but while you are in the dark place, the hidden place, that is the place he prepares you to bloom. John 12:24 says this:

"Unless a kernel of wheat falls to the ground and dies, it remains only a seed. But if it dies, it produces many seeds."

So, rejoice when you feel like death is upon you and you are being hidden! Because God is making sure you don't show up at the party looking like a BUD but rather you show up in FULL BLOOM!

Soaring Requires A Lighter Load

At this point, we know that our hurt and pains have kept us from soaring. They can weigh us down and keep us from taking flight. Sometimes what hurts is not always a result of the offense of others but often the result of our inability to endure the process and move on toward maturation. If we idolize the hurt more than we deal with the real issues, we will do exactly what the enemy wants us to do. He desires that we resign from what matters most in our lives. If we resign from the process, we miss the complete revelation of God and who we are to become.

Revival requires pain identification, which is necessary for healing. Once we grasp firmly that pain masquerades and flaunts itself in our lives in the form of fear, rejection, abandonment, guilt, shame, rebellion, unforgiveness, anger, bitterness, and frustration, etc., then we are more apt not to allow our pain to ground us again. When we are on the potter's wheel, on occasion, fragments of clay, dirt, and foreign objects get thrown into the mix. The potter still maintains the ability to remove what is unnecessary and even reconstruct the clay should it get thrown off the wheel. In many cases, what was intended to destroy us ends up as prosperity and elevation for us. One key to dealing with the things happening inside us is to ensure that we are relentless in our belief that God is constantly working on our behalf. Even when Joseph endured trials and hardship, he came out of it all saying,

> *"But as for you, you meant evil against me; but God meant it for good, in order to bring it about as it is this day, to save many people alive.". (Genesis 50:20) (NKJV)*

Let Go Of The Smoke!

The fieriest trials of our lives can lead us to resign to fight or flight. But for those who have endured fiery trials, why would you let the smoke if the fire didn't kill you? In the story of Shadrach, Meshach, and Abednego, as written in Daniel, 3:27:

> "All the important people, the government leaders and king's counselors, gathered around to examine them and discovered that the fire hadn't so much as touched the three men—not a hair singed, not a scorch mark on their clothes, not even the smell of fire on them". (MSG)

As a lesson from their testimony, "if you made it through the fire, don't let the smoke hang around on your clothes." Long after the fire has ended, many of us still carry the smoke in our clothes to indicate what we have been through. Yes, we were wounded, hurt, and bruised. However, restoration is available to us to overcome every situation we have come through.

In many cases where we have been wounded, what happened shouldn't have happened. The question remains, "How long will you smell like what you have been through?" If I am going to have a testimony, I prefer that I don't look like what I have been through. By all means, I won't come through the fire and still smell like soot. If God brought me through the fire, I intend to look like pure gold and smell like victory.

In our Western construct and thought processes, we've been taught that suffering is a negative experience, and we don't welcome that experience. One advantage we have as believers is that we have a promise at the end of our suffering.

Endure Fiery Trials And Suffering

In the book of 1 Peter, the word suffering is used over 21 times. At this time, Nero had Christians tarred, burned, and then hung in his garden. As a result, Peter had to admonish the people regarding the role that suffering plays alongside our faith. Peter shares in 1 Peter 4:12,

"Dear friends, do not be surprised at the painful trial you are suffering, as though something strange were happening to you".(CEB)

Paul told Timothy in 2 Timothy 3:12: "In fact, everyone who wants to live a godly life in Christ Jesus will be persecuted." (NIV)

God wants us to be free, healed, and made whole. We must override the tendency to hide, deny, or ignore the pain and suffering that we experience. Ultimately, the decision to be delivered is not one that anyone can make for us. Indeed, it's the decision we must make and then follow through with that decision. The reality is that suffering happens in all of our lives. We are not alone in this, and we shouldn't deny the pain of our situations but rather learn to deal wholeheartedly with our experiences.

We don't have to appear as if nothing has happened. However, our stance should be not to allow pain to rule us. When we properly address the matters of our hearts, our pain will enable us to see another aspect of humanity and God while experiencing his love.

Herein lies the greater issue, we can easily be stuck in a place where we play the victim due to our losses. If we play the victim in our story, then we will never fully accept the process of growth and maturation that pain can produce. You can allow your story to be the impetus for growth, or it can be the thing the enemy uses to destroy you.

1 Peter 5:8-11 warns us in this manner, "Keep a cool head. Stay alert. The Devil is poised to pounce, and would like nothing better than to catch you napping. Keep your guard up. You're not the only ones plunged into these hard times. It's the same with Christians all over the world. So, keep a firm grip on the faith. The suffering won't last forever. It won't be long before this generous God who has great plans for us in Christ — eternal and glorious plans they are! — will have you put together and on your feet for good. He gets the last word; yes, he does." (MSG)

God loved us so much that He gave his son as the ultimate sacrifice, the redemption for our sins. We're created in his image, He created us with emotions and feelings. Alongside our innate ability to feel and experience the joy and pains of life, we also have the word of God; a story of redemption, grace, peace, and favor for all mankind who are willing to receive the wisdom contained within.

We may say, "Well, I am not God, I am only human" This is true, but for those of us who have accepted Christ as Lord, we are partakers in grace. As partakers in grace, we have the supernatural ability to experience our pain and overcome our pain. According to Hebrews 12:15,

"See to it that no one fails to obtain the grace of God; that no "root of bitterness" springs up and causes trouble, and by it many become defiled." (ESV)

Our Christian faith is not asking us to deny the pain but rather to wrap our pain in the grace of God and allow that pain to be the experience that propels us closer to Him. Paul, after being imprisoned, still comes out of his experience stating,

"I want to know Christ and the power of his resurrection and the fellowship of sharing in his sufferings, becoming like him in his death, and so, somehow, to attain to the resurrection from the dead." (Philippians 3:10–11) (NIV)

While Psalm 119:71 reminds us, "It was good for me to be afflicted so that I might learn your decrees."(KJV)

Coming Out Of A Stuck Place And Cycles Of Pain

We must learn to forgive ourselves. Forgiveness is necessary for our love to walk. We can deny our experiences or believe a false narrative that agrees with condemnation and our painful experiences to our detriment. Liberty and freedom are contingent upon understanding that whatever has happened to us, forgiveness is available no matter what role we played in the experience. Check where you've blamed yourself for painful situations you didn't create. God desires us to be free from the guilt and the shame of negative circumstances.

John 3:17 reads, "For God did not send His Son into the world to condemn the world, but to save the world through Him." (NIV)

Deal with the pain, but allow it to perfect and refine you instead of stalling your future. Our response to pain should be like this:

> "Since you showed up, I'll do the work required to deal with you."

> " "I'll check myself; I'll look at why I respond to you like I do."

> "I'll soul search and look in the mirror."

> "I won't blame anybody else, but rather deal with the hard realities."

"I'm resigned to do whatever it takes to bring forth freedom in the midst of the situation."

There must be a refusal within to blame others for all of our stuff. They may be sympathetic or empathetic to your pain, but it's not their responsibility to relieve you, nor does it equate to pain acceptance. A relationship becomes toxic when we expect others to bear the burden of our traumatic experiences. From our places of brokenness, we can decide to be bitter, better, wounded, or delivered. The presence of the Lord is one sure place where healing can begin.

The choice is up to you to be made whole and not allow pain to sabotage relationships or create breaches. Ultimately, when your suffering is over, you will leave yourself with great imposition in your relationships if you don't resolve what ails you. In this manner, it's imperative not to play the victim. In doing so, we may find ourselves accepting the enemy's lies of isolation, fear, rejection, etc., which further causes us to stay stuck in a circular pattern of pain. In many cases, our suffering is not the result of suffering or warfare but rather the fruits of disobedience.

One thing that I have learned; no matter what I am going through and what has happened, when I go to God, He causes me to look inwardly. God will not allow us to continue in a pattern of victimization; He leads us towards overcoming instead of the defeatist attitudes that accompany victimization. According to Proverbs 4:23-27 (AMP);

Watch over your heart with all diligence, for from it flows the springs of life. Put away from you a deceitful (lying, misleading) mouth, and put devious lips far from you. Let your eyes look directly ahead [toward the path of moral courage] And let your gaze be fixed straight in front of you [toward the path of integrity]. Consider well and watch carefully the path of your feet, and all your ways will be steadfast and sure. Do not turn away to the right nor to the left [where evil may lurk]; Turn your foot from [the path of] evil.

Recovery from pain, wounds, loss and grief is incumbent upon our ability to fully rely on God's grace, power, and peace to carry us through. Honestly, we pray for things that we often don't want. For instance, we ask for the peace of God that passes all understanding, but when it shows up, we are un-nerved and return the peace that God has granted us.

James 1:8 says, "*a double- minded man is unstable in all his ways.*"

Overcoming Sounds And Looks Like This:

1. I overcome by experiencing the pain, but not letting the pain overcome me.
2. I consciously decide and choose daily to live and to grow closer to God,
3. I take time to look inside, examine myself and to find out who I am.
4. I acknowledge as long as I see self-examination as punishment, I will never mature.
5. I believe accountability and willingness to change is an external character trait required for growth, freedom, and maturity and denies defeat.

Prayer:

Father, today, break the cycle of pain, frustration, fear, trauma, and repetitive behaviors that have hindered my growth and maturation and kept me from taking flight. I guard my heart against any bitterness, unforgiveness, and offense inhibiting my call to soar and rise to the higher place in you that I'm called to.

I acknowledge that you are a God of grace who is not a high priest who cannot empathize with our weaknesses but be tempted in every way without sin. You are not far removed from the matters that plague my heart, but instead, you are available to assist me in guarding my heart and being mindful of the wellspring of life that it is and the issues that proceed from it.

Create in me a clean heart and renew the right spirit within me according to Psalms 51:10. I am ready to release every hindrance so that I can take flight and soar into my destined place!

CHAPTER NINE

Roof Raisers

> *Oh! men and brethren, what would this heart feel if I could but believe that there were some among you who would go home and pray for a revival-men whose faith is large enough, and thier love fiery enough to lead them from this moment to exercice unceasing intercessions that God would appear among us and do wondrous things here, as in the times of former generations.*
>
> C.H SPURGEON

As a revivalist, what you encounter and what has attempted to cause you to be "stuck" in the past may be what God uses to place you on assignment. Your assignment is further confirmed by the "defining" moments that created significant changes in your life. Some moments can shake, make, shift, or shape us, but ultimately it is up to us what we do with them. You have made it thus far. You have counted the costs, did the work, now it's time to raise the roof!

No More Being Stuck, No More Paralysis.

This is the season of defining moments. Your life has qualified you to mark the place of change that promotes, secures, and brings you to the place of elevation. When you are freed from the place of paralysis, you are now able to help someone else get to their "unstuck" place. The issues that we overcome today, God will use tomorrow to assist us in helping someone else.

The story of the paralytic man speaks to a defining moment that changed his life forever.

> Luke 5:18-25(NIV)
>
>> Some men came carrying a paralyzed man on a mat and tried to take him into the house to lay him before Jesus. When they could not find a way to do this because of the crowd, they went up on the roof and lowered him on his mat through the tiles into the middle of the crowd, right in front of Jesus. When Jesus saw their faith, he said, "Friend, your sins are forgiven." The Pharisees and the teachers of the law began thinking to themselves, "Who is this fellow who speaks blasphemy? Who can forgive sins but God alone?" Jesus knew what they were thinking and asked, "Why are you thinking these things in your hearts? Which is easier: to say, 'Your sins are forgiven,' or to say, 'Get up and walk'? But I want you to know that the Son of Man has authority on earth to forgive sins." So he said to the paralyzed man, "I tell you, get up, take your mat and go home." Immediately he stood up in front of them, took what he had been lying on and went home praising God.

Defining Moments

In these defining moments, we're most likely at a place of utter disappointment, frustration, and anxiety over our future and next because hindrances are enlarged in our eyesight. As a result, we fail to see that God comes in this moment not to DESTROY US BUT TO DEFINE US. Our paralysis defined us in times past and identified us as a victim, a liar, a thief, a fornicator, an adulterer, less than imperfect, scorned, insecure, depressed, depraved, victimized, ostracized, rejected, abandoned, and thrown away.

However, this is the moment that you are not destroyed, but you are made! This is the moment that you are not cast off, but you're invited in! This is when you are not exposed to your weakness, but His strength covers you! This is the moment that God says not only will I establish you, but I will birth purpose in you!

When you need to get to Jesus, He will always meet you where you are, but sometimes you may have to ascend to a higher plane to get to Him. You may have to let some folks go because this next season of your life requires that you have people in your corner who understand when to use the roof and not the door. Many of you are in a place where God is elevating you, so the doors you have been using will not work in this next season. You need the roof!

You need to get to Jesus through an unconventional, non-traditional method. Your situation requires that you get to Jesus by any means necessary. He is calling you to a place where you can no longer be amongst those that tolerate, enable, or further embed your paralysis, but they are there to help you be raised above the things that have kept you inhibited in the past.

For many, before you were in a state of paralysis, there was a defining moment, trauma, or circumstance that caused you to experience arrested development. Because of this event or series of events, the enemy robbed you at that place and took away your mobility either by your investment in his lies or your inability to move beyond the moment that came to inhibit, undermine, and dictate a different course of action for your future other than the one God has already spoken to you.

Immobility is truly debilitating because it causes us not to have the full range of motion of our limbs and to be able to move freely. However, it is one thing to be immobile, spiritually or naturally, but a different thing to be paralyzed. Your immobility is a loss of the ease of motion, but paralysis is a state where motion no longer exists in one area. It is one thing to have episodes of immobility and a different thing to be paralyzed.

The enemy desires to keep you paralyzed by your past, by the things you desire to see done differently to the point that you will not be able to advance and move to your "next." He would much rather see you stuck than see you free to become and free to be all God is calling you to become. When you agree with him and operate from the woundedness, the pain of the trial, and the imposition of your situation, you become paralyzed or stuck by that moment. That moment serves to define you not in the way God wants you to be defined but by the negative caricature that the enemy would like you to take on of yourself.

When you decide you're in the place to accept paralysis no longer and being stuck, you get the benefit of Jesus, who is always "passing by" and willing to set us free. Jesus comes not only to deal with what your situation did to you but to free you from the posture of your heart resulting from the situation. So, he says to the paralyzed man. You are forgiven of your sins. The fact that the man was forgiven of his sins produced healing, and he could now take up his bed and walk.

God is trying to get us to the place where we can deal with the condition and the root of what made us stuck in the first place. Because once we deal with the root. The rejection, the fear, the abandonment, the bitterness, the unforgiveness, the failure, the loss, the broken relationships, the hurt, and the pain, then He can at that moment re-define who you are and take you from a stuck person to one who has been made whole. In a moment, God re-defined this man and changed his whole nature. He took him from being the person that had laid on his bed, day after day, nursing his wounds and relying on others to bring him through, to a man that now was able to pick up his mat, his issues, and not be subjugated to them, but to be delivered from him.

Let's go deeper...His mat represented the things that had him bound. Afterward, he was no longer under subjection to his mat. He could carry it, showing he had taken authority over his imposition by the power of God that was now evident in his life. The Pharisees had a problem with Jesus and accused him of blasphemy. However, Jesus related to the man from a place of authority where not only did he forgive him for the penalty of his sins but also for the impact those sins had on his life. He came not only to remove the sin penalty but also to deliver him from their punishment. He tells the man to take up his bed and walk and not only that but to keep walking. God is saying to you in this hour, "Not only will you walk, but you will keep walking."

You are in a season where you will no longer operate as one who is stuck but as one ready to experience the power of God. This power is available to keep walking in your freedom and wholeness. The things that attempted to keep you bound in your last season will no longer have the same power of influence in your life. A new level of freedom is coming upon you to heal you and set you free from the issues of the past.

In times past, we could not be "UNSTUCK" because

we loved our dysfunction. We attracted drama, and we were attracted to drama. Our dysfunction keeps us relevant in our eyes because it allows us to play the victim while remaining at the center of our attention in our stories and others' stories. It's too much to manage when life is normal because we become accustomed to living this way.

Then there were other times when we needed help to navigate the course for what was next. We are in the place where we envision our tomorrow, full of purpose and vision, but we cannot see how to mobilize to the future. Our future dreams and visions seem to be near us but also so far away.

If that's where you are, don't be dismayed! I know it seems that every time you are almost there, something seemingly comes to have you stuck and paralyzed again. However, this is just a reminder that this is a challenge because there is too much discourse around your arrival. You're prepped to arrive at the place God has called you to be and to be used as the revivalist he has now equipped you to be!

What is good about this loss of mobility is simply this; being stuck is the one thing that causes you to feel weak, ill-equipped, insufficient, and insecure about your future. However, the marvelous thing about this narrative is this: "When you are weak, then you are truly strong because His strength is made perfect in weakness." That is when you take hold of a "2 Corinthians 12:8-10 moment" and a DIVINE EXCHANGE. For what you lack, God is making it available to you through His DIVINITY. He is swapping out your weakness for His strength.

It may not feel like it now because, at this exchange, you have already been weakened in your faith and energy, exhausted in your resources, and non-existent in your prayers. Yet what you are facing is equivalent to the strength of 400 men who have come to destroy you inwardly when you are already at the point of tremendous defeat. But here's the main caveat; what paralyzed you also just "SET YOU FREE!"

You didn't expect that the thing that was intended to hurt you was the very same thing that came to set you free. You didn't expect that the death certificate they thought you were about to sign was the very thing that just gave you a new lease on life. You were unaware that had it not been for the death, there would be no need for the resurrection. God extended your contract and gave you new terms.

What was designed to destroy you in the last season wasn't even at the hands of the enemy. It was the thing that God desired to recalibrate you and ensure that when you go over into your land of promise that what looked like it would keep you STUCK, God used as a means for you to encounter Him and to walk again. The things you lost were not a result of the enemy's doing, but God allowed you to see. He would not let you be STUCK by loss because he is your provider. He is the one that is about to reveal to you he can take care of all things concerning you. The friends you lost in this season were not a result of the enemy's doing, but it is the thing that God can use to remind you that He is removing those out of your life that are unnecessary for where he is taking you. He refined your circle so that he could increase your influence.

The warfare you feel in your finances is not always the enemy's doing but could be what God used to get you UNSTUCK. God needed to move you from a place of poverty into wealth and riches. I am no longer mad about the things that were used to keep me stuck in the last season because I know a man who came to me and said, "Take up your bed and walk!"

If it hadn't been for my stuck place, I would have thought that everything I needed I could accomplish. I wouldn't have needed a roof because I would've opened my doors. I would have believed that the medicine they told me to take was responsible for my healing and never experienced God's miraculous power. It is time for us to be like the four friends. We have all had friends who were okay with our imposition, but the revivalist in this hour is willing to help themselves and others to "raise the roof."

Jesus is calling his people in this hour to come out of their state of paralysis and to do whatever it takes to get to a place where they will no longer be stuck by the things that attempted to bind them but be free from the things that have been the hold up to them moving to their next and living life freely. Once the four friends got the man to Jesus, he was not concerned about his natural condition but rather the position of his heart. He spoke to his heart condition and told him his sins were forgiven.

You Are Somebody's Deliverer:

You may not be stuck right now, but maybe God called you to like one of the four friends. You are now able to assist someone through their fight. The warfare being produced in your life today may be the very war God is using to produce a deliverer out of you. It may be the warfare that assures your testimony and causes others to become exactly who God has called them to be. This is the life revivalist are called to. They endure the process, and in doing so, others are made aware of the testimony and come closer to Jesus.

Prayer:

Father, you have established defining moments in my life that are paramount to what you desire to do in and through me! I align my faith with you and war against anything that has held me captive, in bondage, stuck and paralyzed. I am moving to where you desire me to be, and I am no longer bound by (make your confessions here)!

Because I am free, I am now empowered to help others to be free. Thank you, God, for an anointing that I believe is coming over my life and releasing me to move into the dimension and realm of possibilities you have established for me!

I am ready to come out of the box, out of the ordinary, out of the mundane, the lethargic, and stuck places, and move into the extraordinary, the place of beyond, uncommon, and monumental destiny! I am ready to raise the roof!!!

CHAPTER TEN

Worshipping Warriors

Revival is falling in love with Jesus all over again.

VANCE HAVNER

We have greater works to do! Not only are these works greater, but they are also uncommon. The revivalist must be overly acquainted, familiar with, and versed in worship. Worship is more than the dynamics of leading a set worship list at a church service or how we respond to our worship teams during a service. God is calling the Body of Christ on a journey into His presence. Our next destination is a place that demands our focus and attention to be on Him. Revival through the lens of a worshipper requires a renewed desire, passion, hunger, and thirst for God. Revivalists are worshipping warriors. They war and contend against everything attempting to move them away from or out of their destined place of worship.

Remember The One Who Brought You Out

In Deuteronomy 8, God called the Israelites to a place of remembrance. Through Moses, God continually warned them to remember Him and acknowledge the things he had done for them. God admonished them to remember; they would not easily be swayed to worship other gods. When we remember God, we stir revival in our hearts. Worship is an act of acknowledging God's character and His nature. It pushes us to prioritize His stance as the one who is worthy to be honored and adored while placing Him above anything desiring to take priority seating in our lives. There is nothing else we should ascribe worship to. Revival sparks our interest in us remembering Him.

In the early years of my salvation, God dealt with me continually about being a worshipper. While everyone should worship, I sensed a different calling to worship. However, in my heart, I kept saying, "Father, I just want to worship You," yet I struggled with what I thought to be worship was enough. I received prophecy upon prophecy regarding my leading others into worship and how God would use me in that manner. I was around people who were worshippers. Although, I didn't feel qualified as a "worshipper."

I knew I loved God and would give my all to serve him, but I felt something was missing inside. Then the Father revealed that my worship had to go beyond an experience in church, a melodic song, or even an encounter with Him. The heart of a worshipper defines a person who has set their affections on God wholeheartedly and is determined to live a life that acknowledges Him in everything. I had to re-calibrate my thinking to align with the true heart nature of worship from that day forward.

Come Closer

It's easy for us to imitate what we think is worship in our

services, but how many of us go beyond the mechanics/ritual of worship and enter into the position of worship in our day-to-day living? This is the requirement of the revivalist. To present pure, undefiled worship, not by what they do on Sunday morning but by how they live every day.

> *Isaiah 29:13: "The Lord says: "These people come near to me with their mouth and honor me with their lips, but their hearts are far from me. Their worship of me is based on merely human rules they have been taught"*

Because we fail to live a life set apart unto God, we are not easily recognized by the world as being set apart. Consecration is positioning our lives to worship Him. During a season of consecration, we're preparing ourselves to look more like Christ so that more of his glory can be released in us. The world doesn't recognize us because we have not fully positioned ourselves to recognize Jesus through true worship.

We don't just need a week of services that we deem revival. We need revival in our spirits, a renewed interest in worship, and a restored focus on the God we serve. Worship must go beyond our ability to orchestrate words of adoration and engage all our faculties, spirit, soul, and body.
We must set our minds to worship the Lord. Our hearts must be open and free to him when we come into his presence. We may still have issues prevalent in our life before, during, or even after worship, but the most important thing is that we enter and hold nothing back from God.

Circumcised Hearts

Deuteronomy 10:10-15:

> *10And I [Moses] stayed on the mountain, as the first time, forty days and nights, and the Lord listened to me at that*

> *time also; the Lord would not destroy you. 11And the Lord said to me, Arise, journey on before the people, that they may go in and possess the land which I swore to their fathers to give to them. 12And now, Israel, what does the Lord your God require of you but [reverently] to fear the Lord your God, [that is] to walk in all His ways, and to love Him, and to serve the Lord your God with all your [mind and] heart and with your entire being, 13To keep the commandments of the Lord and His statutes which I command you today for your good? 14Behold, the heavens and the heaven of heavens belong to the Lord your God, the earth also, with all that is in it and on it. 15Yet the Lord had a delight in loving your fathers, and He chose their descendants after them, you above all peoples, as it is this day. 16So circumcise the foreskin of your [minds and] hearts; be no longer stubborn and hardened.*

The Lord commanded the Israelites to circumcise (cut away all the excess, the unnecessary part) their hearts. The cutting away of the useless things from their heart freed them to worship Him. They had not positioned themselves in a place of total engagement in worship. They still held on to a stubborn and hardened attitude forsaking a pure heart posture towards God. In order to enter into a worship relationship with God, we have to cut away all the unnecessary parts. Everything that hinders us from entering into this relationship with him must go.

> *Deuteronomy 11:16: "Take heed to yourselves, lest your [minds and] hearts be deceived and you turn aside and serve other gods and worship them."*

Everybody in our world worships something; however, we are to worship God only. We can't be deceived by our own hearts to think that we worship God simply because we are Christians. We have to make a solid decision to become a worshipper, or else we will turn to other gods to worship, resulting in idolatry. Idolatry is a critical issue in our generation, many worship their own lives, ideals, success, and the like while removing God from the equation. In the church, we see people worship ministries, leaders, titles, and positions relating to or pertaining to Christianity; but they don't truly worship God.

Worship Is Not Performance

Worship is relational and intimate. It's between you and God. No one can dictate how you worship God, just like no one can dictate how to be intimate with your spouse. There are methods and principles of worship, but your encounter with Him is relational and intimate. However, worship does require that you engage all of you both in the act (physical) of worship and the lifestyle of worship.

Ephesians 3:19: "[That you may really come] to know [practically, through experience for yourselves] the love of Christ, which far surpasses mere knowledge [without experience]; that you may be filled [through all your being] unto all the fullness of God [may have the richest measure of the divine Presence, and become a body wholly filled and flooded with God Himself".

The Apostle Paul said that he desired for the Body of Christ to become intimately acquainted with God. The intimacy that God wants from us is one on one. It's not written in a step-by-step manual, the manner in which we learn the love of God, because he shows us his love through relationship on an individual basis. There are certain things that are relevant to us all about his love, like the fact that he died for us, there's no greater love than that. However, his love for us must become experiential.

The word "worship" is derived from the Anglo-Saxon word Weorthscipe- "worth" and "ship," which means one worthy of reverence and honor. Worship is the celebration of God's supreme worth in such a manner that God's worthiness becomes the norm and inspiration of human living. (Ralph Martin-The Worship of God). Fellowship is when you are in the face of God, seeking him and communing with Him. But worship begins when you get off your face and consciously decide to do what God has told you to do because worship is an act of your obedience.

True Worship Presents The Entire Life To God

A true worshipper dedicates his life to God's will, purpose, and plan. A true worshipper decides to live according to the precepts and ordinances God has outlined in his word. When you worship God, you don't have difficulty figuring out His will for your life. You will know his will by asking, "Is the decision I'm making bringing me closer to God and causing me to be more like him?" The will of God for every believer is to have their mind transformed and renewed so that they will emulate Christ.

> *Romans 12:1: I appeal to you therefore, brethren, and beg of you in view of [all] the mercies of God, to make a decisive dedication of your bodies [presenting all your members and faculties] as a living sacrifice, holy (devoted, consecrated) and well pleasing to God, which is your reasonable (rational, intelligent) service and spiritual worship. Do not be conformed to this world (this age), {fashioned after and adapted to its external, superficial customs} but be transformed (changed) by the {entire} renewal of your mind {by its new ideal and its new attitude}, so that you may prove what is the good and acceptable and perfect will {in His sight for you.*

Authentic worship is entering into a place of "yes." A place where we desire to please God and not ourselves. A place where we are sensitive to ensuring his goals and priority is met on earth. Authentic worship is kingdom work. Authentic worship is being and doing what God has called us to be. It's putting your hands on the plow and not looking back. Our worship has to go farther than an experience with Him. Just one encounter with Him will change our lives, but if we encounter Him and don't allow that change to operate in us, then the encounter profits us little.

Do You See Him?

> *John 4:19: The woman said to Him, Sir, I see and understand that You are a prophet. Our forefathers worshiped on this mountain, but you [Jews] say that Jerusalem is the place where it is necessary and proper to worship. Jesus said to her, Woman, believe Me, a time is coming when you will worship the Father neither [merely] in this mountain nor [merely] in Jerusalem. You [Samaritans] do not know what you are worshiping [you worship what you do not comprehend]. We do know what we are worshiping [we worship what we have knowledge of and understand], for [after all] salvation comes from [among] the Jews. A time will come, however, indeed it is already here, when the true (genuine) worshipers will worship the Father in spirit and in truth (reality); for the Father is seeking just such people as these as His worshipers. God is a Spirit (a spiritual Being) and those who worship Him must worship Him in spirit and in truth (reality). The woman said to Him, I know that Messiah is coming, He Who is called the Christ (the Anointed One); and when He arrives, He will tell us everything we need to know and make it clear to us. The woman said to Him, I know that Messiah is coming, He Who is called the Christ (the Anointed One); and when He arrives, He will tell us everything we need to know and make it clear to us. Jesus said to her, I Who now speak with you am He.*

Spirit And Truth In Worship

Jesus is telling this woman that there will be a time where the importance of where we worship will not be the issue. The issue will become that when you worship, and rather you understand who you worship. Jesus informs the women that the Samaritans did not even know who they were worshipping. They worshipped something that they had no knowledge of. God is seeking worshippers who know who he is in reality and truth. Even after this discussion, the Samaritan woman was unaware she was speaking to Jesus. She spoke to him about himself as if he wasn't even there.

Jesus was dealing with the fact that there is no need to debate where we worship God. Because there is a time when worship will not be confined to a building because we will build our lives on worship and consistently be in worship. We will worship Him in spirit by being obedient to the Spirit of God, and we will worship Him in truth by receiving a greater revelation of Him through his word as we yield to Him.

Worship should become second nature to us. Worship should be who we are and what we do. Our constant position must be, "I belong to God, and I am here to do what he has called me to do." When we fail to live a life set apart unto God, we are not easily recognized by the world. Consecration is positioning our lives to worship him. During a season of consecration, we prepare ourselves to look more like Him so that more of his glory can be released in us.

Mark The Place And Worship Him There

Genesis 22:13-14 (Jehovah Jireh)

Then Abraham looked up and glanced around, and behold, behind him was a ram caught up in a thicket by his horns.

And Abraham went and took the ram and offered it up for a burnt offering and an ascending sacrifice instead of his Son! Abraham called the name for that place THE LORD WILL PROVIDE. And it is said to this day, On the mount of the Lord it will be provided.

We have to mark the place where God shows up in our lives. We must be aware of what God is doing in our lives at certain times and places. We don't want to offer up one-dimensional worship to God. But as we see him operative in our lives, we must be aware of who He reveals Himself to us and then worship Him from that place. The world will see Christ through a worshipper because their lives emulate Him.

This season of worship that the church is entering into has much less to do with music, as it does transformation and changed lives. The revivalist will not only enter the presence of God and come out changed but they will also come out carrying a weight of His glory that is conducive for a move of God. These individuals will be empowered and equipped to shift atmospheres, interrupt cultures, empower environments with His presence, and experience miracles, signs, and wonders as a usual occurrence. As a result, many will come to the kingdom and commit to the cause of Christ.

Prayer:

Father, you require a pure and circumcised heart for worship, so I align my desire with yours today. If I have a stony heart, I pray today that you will give me a heart of flesh. Release me to function from a place of reckless abandon to your will, your way, and purity of heart in living a life of worship unto you.

As a revivalist, the transformation of my heart is my pursuit, and I renounce any challenge (insert the challenge here) to my ability to be free to worship you in spirit and truth. Revival requires the pure-hearted worshippers, not the entertainers, not the performers, not the attention-seekers, and I require what you require.

I denounce any element of self-glory or vain ambition that has crept into my worship and pray that you will release the sound of pure worship and the fragrance of true worship through a life of surrender to you. I am submitted to you and desire to see the fullness of your glory exhibited within! Let my worship be pleasing and honorable to you in the sanctuary, the marketplace, the field, my home, and wherever I may be. Clouds and clouds of glory follow me, and revival is produced through me as I worship you!

CHAPTER ELEVEN

Uncommon Revivalists

The story of revivals throughout the ages has been the story of lone men meeting God, of going out and finding God all alone. Sometimes they went down to the church basement, sometimes to the caves, sometimes out under trees, sometimes by haystacks, but they went alone to meet God, and then the revival went out from there.

A.W. TOZER

When we study the life of Jesus, there was not much that was common, routine, practical, ordinary, or traditional about His methods. As we follow His life, we see that his ministerial goal was never set upon his location, a building, a temple, or a synagogue. Still, He lived His life in such a manner that wherever He was, the ministry was to follow. When He stepped on the scene, atmospheres shifted, lives changed, and people encountered something they had never experienced. So it is with the revivalists God is calling you to a place to impact others in the same manner as He did.

John 14:12 tells us, "Verily, verily, I say unto you, He that believeth on me, the works that I do shall he do also; and greater works than these shall he do; because I go unto my Father." (KJV)

We have greater works to do! Not only are these works greater, but they are also uncommon. Jesus had no fear in ministry. He ministered to those who were not always doing the right thing, nor had all their p's and q's together. He served a community of people who appeared to be disenfranchised, out of bounds, and maybe not even necessary—among that list included Ten Lepers, Zacchaeus the Tax Collector, The Woman with the Alabaster Box, The Woman at the Well, and so many more. Still, typically these were not the well-to-do or those considered popular or to have had everything together.

Discipleship

Another common thread of the Life of Jesus is that he realized the art of replication, multiplication, and impartation. He considered that if he had a few good men on his team, he could invest in their life and that they would, in turn, do the work they were called to do.

In that manner, He took a group of men with different temperaments and vocations and turned their impossibilities into possibilities. In the true nature of a carpenter, He crafted these individuals into spiritual giants and those who would walk with him while he took the world by storm.

Jesus was not big on doing church as usual. While we see him occasionally teaching in the synagogue, He was typically found doing ministry in places where ministry was not likely to happen. He did things like turning up at parties or weddings by turning water into wine, on boats when people's lives were in danger, in fields where people were seemingly isolated and alone, and on the roadside, where people traveled. He went into folks' homes and met people on the mountainside and by the side of the lake. He was not limited in his ministry scope and sought opportunities to be a blessing.

The ministry of Jesus was about something other than the size of a building, location, financial gain, ministerial prestige, or the like. He ministered because He wanted to see people experience changed lives and get to the heart of what hindered them from doing so. He confronted the needs of people and met them at the point of their needs. In true form, this is the mandate of revivalists. It is also the mandate of Uncommon Church. As a revivalist, my husband and I are concerned about returning to a place where we do what Jesus did. This should be the goal of every church, but that is not the case.

We have said for so long no longer church as usual. However, we continue to pattern church after all the irrelevant things for preparing the bride of Christ for its soon-coming king. As the church, we must find a way to break out of our mindsets, our ways of thinking about and doing church, and do church in an uncommon manner. We pattern our church after this model, not just so we appear as if we are different, but rather as an effort to be more like Jesus truly. If we are honest, we see less of Jesus and more of everything else in our churches today.

God is raising uncommon venues, spaces, and ways for church so the unsaved can experience Christ. Being uncommon or a revivalist does not mean a lack of structure, order, or protocol, but it applies to those who desire to be spirit-led in whatever they do. God uses ordinary people empowered by an extraordinary God to accomplish Uncommon things on Earth. (Uncommon Church Motto).

John 4:1-52 reads, "Now Jesus learned that the Pharisees had heard that he was gaining and baptizing more disciples than John—although in fact it was not Jesus who baptized, but his disciples. So he left Judea and went back once more to Galilee. Now he had to go through Samaria. So he came to a town in Samaria called Sychar, near the plot of ground Jacob had given to his son Joseph. Jacob's well was there, and Jesus, tired as he was from the journey, sat down by the well. It was about noon.

When a Samaritan woman came to draw water, Jesus said to her, "Will you give me a drink?" (His disciples had gone into the town to buy food.) The Samaritan woman said to him, "You are a Jew and I am a Samaritan woman. How can you ask me for a drink?" (For Jews do not associate with Samaritans.[a]) Jesus answered her, "If you knew the gift of God and who it is that asks you for a drink, you would have asked him and he would have given you living water." "Sir," the woman said, "you have nothing to draw with and the well is deep.

Where can you get this living water? Are you greater than our father Jacob, who gave us the well and drank from it himself, as did also his sons and his livestock?" Jesus answered, "Everyone who drinks this water will be thirsty again, but whoever drinks the water I give them will never thirst. Indeed, the water I give them will become in them a spring of water welling up to eternal life." The woman said to him, "Sir, give me this water so that I won't get thirsty and have to keep coming here to draw water." He told her, "Go, call your husband and come back."

"I have no husband," she replied. Jesus said to her, "You are right when you say you have no husband. The fact is, you have had five husbands, and the man you now have is not your husband. What you have just said is quite true."

"Sir," the woman said, "I can see that you are a prophet. Our ancestors worshiped on this mountain, but you Jews claim that the place where we must worship is in Jerusalem." "Woman," Jesus replied, "believe me, a time is coming when you will worship the Father neither on this mountain nor in Jerusalem. You Samaritans worship what you do not know; we worship what we do know, for salvation is from the Jews. Yet a time is coming and has now come when the true worshipers will worship the Father in the Spirit and in truth, for they are the kind of worshipers the Father seeks. God is spirit, and his worshipers must worship in the Spirit and in truth."

The woman said, "I know that Messiah" (called Christ) "is coming. When he comes, he will explain everything to us." Then Jesus declared, "I, the one speaking to you—I am he." Just then his disciples returned and were surprised to find him talking with a woman. But no one asked, "What do you want?" or "Why are you talking with her?" Then, leaving her water jar, the woman went back to the town and said to the people, "Come, see a man who told me everything I ever did. Could this be the Messiah?" They came out of the town and made their way toward him. Meanwhile his disciples urged him, "Rabbi, eat something." But he said to them, "I have food to eat that you know nothing about." Then his disciples said to each other, "Could someone have brought him food?"

"My food," said Jesus, "is to do the will of him who sent me and to finish his work. Don't you have a saying, 'It's still four months until harvest'? I tell you, open your eyes and look at the fields! They are ripe for harvest. Even now the one who reaps draws a wage and harvests a crop for eternal life, so that the sower and the reaper may be glad together. Thus the saying 'One sows and another reaps' is true. I sent you to *reap what you have not worked for. Others have done the hard work, and you have reaped the benefits of their labor." Many of the Samaritans from that town believed in him because of the woman's testimony, "He told me everything I ever did."*

So when the Samaritans came to him, they urged him to stay with them, and he stayed two days. And because of his words many more became believers. They said to the woman, "We no longer believe just because of what you said; now we have heard for ourselves, and we know that this man really is the Savior of the world." (NIV)

In the text, we see that Jesus is having to deal with the Pharisees, who were jealous because he was baptizing more folks than John the Baptist. At that point, Jesus decides to leave Judea and head towards Galilee. Now because the Jews despised the Samaritans it was customary not to go the direct route to Samaria but preferred to avoid Samaria all together by crossing over the Jordan and traveling on the Eastern Side. However, Jesus was prompted that he had a "MUST NEED." He felt that it was necessary for him to travel through Samaria. Now Samaria was actually the most direct route. And Jesus was determined to do His Father's will and please Him. The truth is that there was a woman at the well that Jesus had a divine appointment with.

1. What do you do when the Father asks you to go to the route that may be the most direct but it's not the normal route? Nobody else is going this way, nobody else likes to travel this way, this is not the popular way to do it, and this way is not the most successful. Nobody likes this way. But still, the Father wants you to travel this route, this way, this road. What do you do?

2. What do you do when God asks you to go a way that may be the most direct route, but on the way, you may be confronted with some folks and some things that you don't want to confront? There are some things in our lives that, if we could go around them and not have to take them head-on, that would be our approach. We don't want to have to speak to the issue. We don't want to have to consider the opposition. We don't want to have to forgive, release, and let go. We would rather go a long way around it so that we don't have to deal with the thing in front of us demanding our attention and response. Avoidance is always preferable, but it is not necessarily what God requires. What do you do when what He requires causes you to confront things you desire not to confront?

3. What do you do when God is asking you to take the most direct route because there is a "MUST NEEDS" situation that he is calling you to? Jesus dedicated his life to ministry and was willing to say yes to whatever the Father required. And in some cases, or most cases, ministry requires sacrifice. Although it was the most direct route, we found it easier to go around some things because, on the direct route, it is straight and narrow, which means we can't skirt the issue, and ultimately some things must die. We don't have time to play games on the direct route because somebody on the other side needs us. We can't keep saying, "I'll get to that tomorrow because, on the direct route, somebody's time of deliverance is now."

The direct route will cost you something because you can't play games on that road. This is not the easiest road. It may require you to sacrifice, but once you realize it, you may meet a "Samaritan," one that is not in your corner, per se, but one that is in need of your ministry. That is the road you need to take, which may be "uncommon."

To Be Uncommon Means:
1. You must be willing to risk taking the popular route in order to fulfill the Kingdom mandate.
2. You must accept that being a pioneer, trailblazer, revolutionist will cause you to be an affront to old paradigms and a creator for new ones.
3. You must be willing to be obedient to the point of sacrifice. Ministry and sacrifice go hand in hand.

To be a revivalist is to be uncommon. It simply means that you will have to take some paths that others desire not to travel. Some took a path that did not yield sacrifice but rather compromise. Some took a path that was not concerned about building God's kingdom but building their kingdom. Some took a path that looked like a direct route, but because it was wrong, it took them out of what and where God was calling them.

It is your time to rise to the occasion, take your position and soar, Revivalist! You are marked. You are necessary and needful for the advancement of the Kingdom of God. The clarion call you to feel requires you to separate from everything hindering your coming forth.

Instead of being hindered, receive God's love and desire to use you as an agent of change and transformation on the earth! You are a container for His glory, and as healing takes place, He is replacing the wounds with His power and glory. You are not only called but called to the kingdom for such a time as this! Don't disregard your unique qualities, character, and abilities. God is taking what you may think is "uncommon" and using it to build an exceeding great army of revivalists!

The Uncommon Revivalist Comes To Grip With

This Statement Of Belief:

I have no idea of all of what God will do in and through me, nor have I seen and envisioned all the possibilities. However, I am committed to doing the will of God in the way that I see Jesus doing it, and for that, I am willing to be uncommon. I AM REVIVAL"!!!

Prayer:

There is a place you are calling me to that is not usual, it's not normal, it's not ordinary, and I am here for it all, Father! I am moving out of the box and the restraints I have placed on my life as I follow the model of Jesus and interrupt paradigms everywhere I go to see the kingdom of God advance.

I expect to see miracles, I expect to see signs, and I expect to see wonders. I expect it all not because I am a seeker of the supernatural but because I expect to see greater works and the demonstration of your power as your word has already declared!

I am not fearful of the path you have laid out for my life. I am on that path and move with accelerated speed and increased capacity to facilitate your will! I am not delayed, denied, or hindered, but I am firmly rooted, established, and operating in grace and favor today! I am ready to boldly declare from the mountains high that "I am revival"!

I am called into the kingdom for such a time of this as I

believe to see your glory revealed in me! I declare it loudly, decree it boldly. I am not becoming, contemplating, nor considering it, but "I AM REVIVAL"!

God, your clarion call has captivated me and produced a passion within to see the kingdoms of this world become the kingdoms of my lord and his Christ, and you, Lord, will reign forever and ever.....AMEN!!!! So it is, and so shall it be!!

FOURTEEN DAYS OF REVIVAL PRAYER

To further your journey take the next 14 days and commit to fasting anf prayer and journaling any insight, revelation or simply what you hear as you spend time in the presence of the Lord.

Let the statement below be your daily declaration:

As a revivalist, I lend myself to God to be used by Him as an agent of change and transformation on the earth. As I prepare to move into deeper dimensions of prayer, I posture myself first for heart transformation and revival within

Day One-I turn away from the areas of sin and unrepentant places in my life that I have not allowed to be touched by the cleansing power of God. Matthew 4:17, Acts 3:19, Acts 20:2

Day Two -I decree that my mind is strengthened and fortified today. God reveals every area where I have not allowed the yoke destroying anointing and power of God to dismantle every issue, weight, chain, fetter, and proclivity of my flesh. Psalm 139:23, Psalm 51:10-13, Isaiah 10:27

Day Three-Recalibrate me! Align me to your will, purposes, and plan for my life. Reveal, dispose of, transform, and renew me until I look like and I'm conformed to the original intention of your will, purpose, and plan for my life. Psalm 143:10

_____

_____

_____

_____

_____

_____

_____

_____

_____

_____

Day Four: There is nothing I will allow to separate me from fully engaging God in spirit and truth. I desire for my life to be pleasing to you, Lord.

I posture my life to be integral, full of truth and character, and one through which God's love can manifest. I am an agent of change and postured to serve you all the days of my life. John 4:24

_____

_____

_____

_____

_____

_____

_____

_____

_____

_____

Day Five -Show me the areas in my life that I have not surrendered to you and allow your divine governance to overthrow every place I have not surrendered.

Nothing in my bloodline, heritage, and lineage will cause me to live below the standard of your will. Your will is my desire. Romans 12:12, Galatians 2:20, Luke 9:23-24

_____

_____

_____

Day Six - I align my mind, soul, spirit, and body to be an offering unto you, Lord, as I desire to serve you in a pleasing manner. All I have is yours, and as you transform me, I am becoming more like you.

I represent you on the earth and desire to be an influence and kingdom ambassador that moves the agenda of heaven forward.
1 Thessalonians 5:23

Day Seven-I decree and declare that today is the dawning of a new day, and I am stepping into my season of divine alignment, purpose, favor, and prominence.

God is transforming my heart in preparation for doing His will and showing forth His glory on the earth. I am a glory carrier, and his light shines through me. Isaiah 43:18-19, Isaiah 60:1, Matthew 5:14-16

Day Eight- I'm seated in heavenly places, and I take my rightful position now as I walk in the full armor of God. Ephesians 2:6-7, Ephesians 6:10.

I wrestle not against flesh and blood but against evil forces, the rulers, authorities, and powers of the kingdom of darkness and spiritual forces of evil in the heavenly realms.Ephesians 6:12-13.

I put on the full armor of God according to Ephesians 6:10-18 with the belt of truth and the breastplate of righteousness that solidifies my standing as I move towards becoming the uncompromisingly righteous and my belief that the just shall live by faith. My feet are ready to carry the gospel of peace today.

I take up the shield of faith to extinguish all the enemy's fiery darts. The Helmet of Salvation is placed upon my head, and I gather the Sword of the Spirit, which is the word of God, as I release his word over my life.

_____

_____

_____

_____

_____

_____

_____

_____

_____

_____

_____

Day Nine-The spirit of fear, disunity, and dishonor is broken in my life today. The spirit of sabotage, contention, and dissension is dismantled, and I have no power of authority over me.

I believe my life will stand to exhibit the miraculous power of God in demonstration and with power. I believe you for a greater manifestation of glory, power, and presence in my life daily. 1 Corinthians 2:4-5

Day Ten-I believe that the heavens are now open and from them comes sustainable increase, wealth, streams of blessing, favor, healing, and glory! Philippians 4:19, Psalm 5:12, Psalm 90:17, Psalm 106:4, 2 Corinthians 9:8 The law of reciprocity and favor works continually and in full operation in my life. Luke 6:38

Day Eleven- I wholeheartedly agree that miracles, signs, and wonders shall be performed in and through me by the divine assistance of Holy Spirit. Hebrews 2:4, Mark 6:17, John 14:12

Day Twelve_The anointing to breakthrough is made available to me now and every spirit that would attempt to prevent breakthrough is brought under the subjection of the power of God. Isaiah 60:1-22, Acts 1:8, Micah 2;13, 2 Samuel 5:20

Day Thirteen-You are bringing me around the right company of people and after being in their presence I will leave their presence as a changed man. (1 Samuel 10) The blood of Jesus covers and seals my life today and protects me from anything that would do me harm. Hebrews 9:14, 1 John 1:7, Matthew 26:28

Day Fourteen-The power of God is given full reign to heal, set free and deliver in any area in my life where healing, freedom, and deliverance is required.

I am recalibrated, restored, reset, reestablished, and reconfirmed in my identify and my purpose and I live to see the manifestation of God's glory in and through me.

I am a son of God and its my pleasure to be revealed in the earth as one! Hebrews 1:3, Colossians 2:12, Romans 15:13, Ephesians 3:20, 2 Timothy 1:7, 2 Peter 1:3, Romans 8:19

REFERENCES

CHAPTER TWO

Metanoeo-New Testament Greek Lexicon-New American Standard. (n.d.). Retrieved January 19, 2019, from https://www.biblestudytools.com/lexicons/greek/nas/metanoeo.html

Epistrepho-New Testament Greek Lexicon-King James Version. (n.d.). Retrieved January 19, 2019, from https://www.biblestudytools.com/lexicons/greek/kjv/epistrepho.html

Finney, Charles. "Revival Sayings and Revival Quotes | Wise Old Sayings." Revival Sayings and Revival Quotes| Wise Old Sayings, www.wiseoldsayings.com/revival-quotes/

Robinson, Lee. "23 Spiritually Invigorating Revival Quotes." Viral Believer, 21 June 2019, www.viralbeliever.com/revival-quotes/.

CHAPTER THREE

Calibrate. (n.d.). Retrieved January 21, 2019, from https://www.merriam-webster.com/dictionary/calibrate.

Recalibrate. (n.d.). Retrieved January 21, 2019, from https://www.merriam-webster.com/dictionary/recalibrate

Ravenhill, Leonard. "Revival Sayings and Revival Quotes | Wise Old Sayings."Revival Sayings and Revival Quotes | Wise Old Sayings, www.wiseoldsayigns.com/revival-quotes/.

CHAPTER FOUR

Emergent. (n.d.). Retrieved January 21, 2019, from https://www.merriam-webster.com/dictionary/emergent

Ravenhill, Leonard. "Leonard Ravenhill Quote; "As Long as We Are Content to LIve without Revival, We Will." Quotefancy, quotefancy.com/qute/852390/Leonard-Ravenhill-As-long-as-we-are-content-to-live-without-revival-we-will.

CHAPTER FIVE

1 Corinthians 13 Commentary - Adam Clarke Commentary. (n.d.). Retrieved January 21, 2019, from https://www.studylight.org/commentaries/acc/1-corinthians-13.html

Spurgeon, Charles. "A Quote from Morning and Evening, bases on the English Standard Version. " Goodreads, Goodreads, www.goodreads.com/quotes/208663-nothing-teaches-us-about-the-preciousness-of-the-creator-as.

CHAPTER SIX

Desert Definition and Meaning - Bible Dictionary. (n.d.). Retrieved January 21, 2019, from https://www.biblestudytools.com/dictionary/desert/
Adrian Rogers Quote: "Study the History of Revival. God Has Always Sent Revival in the Darkest Days. Oh, for a Mighty Sweeping Revival Today!"." Quotefancy, quotefancy.com/quote/1528032/Adrian-Rogers-Study-the-history-of-revival-God-has-always-sent-revival-in-the-darkest.

CHAPTER SEVEN

(n.d.). "Shalom" Retrieved January 21, 2019, from https://biblehub.com/hebrew/7965.html.

CHAPTER EIGHT

Booth, Mary. "Revival Quotes." BEAUTIFUL FEET, romans1015.com/rev-quotes/.

CHAPTER NINE

Finney, Charles. "Revival Sayings and Revival Quotes | Wise Old Sayings." Revival Sayings and Revival Quotes | Wise Old Sayings, www.wiseoldsayings.com/revial-quotes.com

CHAPTER TEN

Havner, Vancfe. "Vance Havner Quote." "A, www.azquotes.com/quote/1035247.

Martin, Ralph. "The Worship of God: Some Theological, Pastoral, and Practical Reflections." Amazon, Amzon, 12 July 1982, www.amazon.com/Worship-God-Theological-Practical-Reflections/dp/0803819346.

CHAPTER ELEVEN

Tozer, A. W., and James L. Syner. The Crucified Life: How to Live Out a Deeper Christian Experience Bethany House, 2014.

ABOUT THE AUTHOR

Dana M. Blue

pray | preach | prophesy | activate | equip | worship

Dana Blue accepted her call to ministry at nineteen and has continued to minister since her early 20s. She graduated from Liberty University with a Master's Degree in Pastoral Counseling & Discipleship Ministries, and she's working towards completing her doctoral degree. The anointing on Dana's life flows along the prophetic spectrum, specifically in prayer, worship, and teaching. In the capacity of a revivalist, she looks forward to "hosting the presence of God" in atmospheres conducive to changed lives. She has also been mandated to train, equip, and activate Emerging Prophetic leaders, Intercessors, Levites, and Believers to effectively demonstrate their prophetic assignment on the earth. She is also the author of I Am Revival: Preparation Guide for Revival Ready People and A.W.A.R.E, a book for women emerging in ministry.

For more information visit: www.danablueministries.com

Photo Credit: J.R. Roseborough Charlotte NC

BOOKS BY THIS AUTHOR

A.w.a.r.e: Empowerment Keys For Women In Ministry

A.W.A.R.E: Empowerment Keys for Women in Ministry assist those who sense the call to ministry to awaken to their potential and to press into their ministerial destiny. A.W.A.R.E is for a generation of AUTHENTIC WOMEN who are AWAKENED, RESTORED, & EQUIPPED. In order to produce the full potential of what resides in us, we must first be AWARE of who we are so that we may ASSESS our dormant potential, and yield ourselves to the ACCESS granted by the Holy Spirit! The outcome allows us to become who God has authentically created and equipped us to be!

Prophetic Stewardship: Tools For Navigating Your Prophetic Journey, Assignment And Mantle

The manner in which we administer a skill, talent, gift, or anointing is increasingly important in this hour. For many prophetic people, the focus has been more on using the gift rather than developing or building a strong basis of theological excellence, character development, and emotional intelligence at the core of the individual's life. This book will help ensure that prophets and prophetic people take seriously the call and requirement to steward effectively their calling to the prophetic dimension. There is a call back to purity, integrity, and the altar for prophetic leaders. This book will assist emerging leaders specifically with tools as they navigate the journey to be better invested in prophetic stewardship.

A.W.A.R.E: Empowerment Key for Women in Ministry

PRAISE FOR AUTHOR

This book is amazing! Let revival break out in our hearts, our homes, schools, jobs, and throughout this world!!! Pastor Dana Blue so eloquently captures the essence of what revival is and what it really and truly means to be revived!!! This is ABSOLUTELY A GOOD READ!!

- NIKEEYA ALI

So far, I've read half of this book and it's been so impactful! I could have finished it already, but I keep going back and re-reading chapters because it's just that good.

The author has written in such a way that it feels like I'm sitting in my living room, having a one on one conversation with her about the inward workings of revival in the hearts of those willing to pay the price for true transformation.

As I read more, I received clarity on things I experienced as early as my childhood on up through the present.... while at the same time presented with what's necessary for me to reach the next level of transformational impact.

This book inspired me. It intrigued me. It challenged me. It ignited me. I highly recommend this book along with her other publication;

A.W.A.R.E.: Empowerment Keys for Women in Ministry!

- PASTORS EMMANUEL AND ADRIENNE THREATT

www.ingramcontent.com/pod-product-compliance
Lightning Source LLC
Chambersburg PA
CBHW022131080426
42734CB00006B/320